WE'LL MEET AGAIN

An Excerpt from the Story of Mr. & Mrs. Rat

JOHN C LAWES

Tellwell Talent
www.tellwell.ca

ISBN
978-0-2288-4106-7 (Hardcover)
978-0-2288-4105-0 (Paperback)
978-0-2288-4107-4 (eBook)

For my wife, Louise

Dearest Louise,

The story recorded here is based mostly upon the altogether too true, too real life experiences of my beloved parents as recorded in my father's Official War Diaries and my mother's correspondence with her parents in Hamilton, Ontario, during World War II. I inherited these documents, along with a collection of tiny, faded, black-and-white photographs and other memorabilia, and saw them for the first time shortly after my mother died in 1991.

I confess I did not cope well with losing my mother. It took me the better part of five years to muster the courage even to look at the bequeathed diaries and letters in any detail. Revelations abounded and impacted me far more deeply than I could ever have anticipated. But would you believe it? I then took only two weeks to write the first draft of this novel. But I have been revisiting and revising it for several years now, searching for the right words, the best balance between story-telling and the grim realities...

Ah, hell—it's not perfect, but it will serve. The place names are real, and most of the events depicted transpired substantially as represented. Names of our immediate family members are genuine, as are those of famous politicians, generals, and entertainers... and the nickname of my father's first batman, 'Nobby.' The names of all other characters are purely fictitious. In particular, when it comes to two characters called Cecil and Walter, I have exercised creative license unabashedly.

Mr. Rat

Mrs. Rat

BARI, ITALY
April 1, 1944

She helped him climb in behind the wheel of the lorry he had commandeered for the evening, ran around, and climbed in beside him. He started the engine, depressed the clutch, and put it in gear. They moved off smoothly. Even in his obviously intoxicated condition, driving was almost second nature. In an unfamiliar city under blackout conditions, however, seeing where he was going was another matter entirely.

"Are you sure you know where you're going, Mr. Rat?" she asked. "It's pitch black out there!"

It was three or four o'clock in the morning. A cool, dense fog clung to their clothes, their skin, and the windscreen, obscuring the view and restricting vision to perhaps ten feet. No moon or stars showed to provide even a hint of light. There were no streetlamps. There was no light spilling from the windows of the nearby buildings, no other vehicles on the road. And, the headlights of the vehicle they were in were not, by design and by order, illuminated.

"Not to worry, Mrs. Rat," he replied, although it sounded more like "*nawdhoowurrhy mizzizzraght.*" He took a drag on his cigarette and turned to smile at her. "'f we go too farrh *oouest* we shtar' goin' *up!* 'f we go too farrh *easht* we shtar' goin' *dowwwn!*" He shifted up through the gears and accelerated. "'Shlong as we stay on lev'l groun'," he turned to smile at her again, "we *cann-nott*' possibly go wrong! *Truss* me!"

At that point, the three-tonne lorry shot out over the end of the dock and into the Adriatic Sea.

CONTENTS

PART 2
TOCCATA

PART 3
FUGUE

PART 1

OVERTURE

1

NORBURY AVENUE, LONDON, ENGLAND
August 1939

"We knew it was coming," said Violet, "but I had hoped it would not be so soon." She looked up beseechingly into the eyes of her husband, Charlie, as he put his arm around her shoulders and drew her to him.

"Now, now dear," he soothed, smiling down at her. "Our boy will be perfectly all right. Won't you, Toddy?" he prodded, raising his eyes to fix his son with a stern regard. It wasn't a question. It was a command.

Harold Stanley Lawes, affectionately called 'Toddy' by his family, had just received his call up. He had voluntarily joined the Territorial Army back in April – just before the bill for limited conscription was introduced in Parliament – and now the telegram had come posting him officially to unit 513 of the Royal Army Service Corps (RASC).

Standing there in the parlor of his parents' house on Norbury Avenue, dressed in the khaki uniform he had been issued by the Quartermaster only last week, he felt proud and confident. Proud to be serving his country. Proud to be following in his father's footsteps. Charlie had served with a Lewis Gun company in The Great War. And confident because, well, mainly because youth and inexperience are close relatives of confidence.

Besides, there was a whole new world out there waiting to be discovered over the next few months.

Drawing his five-foot nine-inch frame up to the position of 'Attention', Harold looked first to his mother Violet, her gray-green eyes brimming with tears, her brow furrowed in concern, and gave her a smile and a wink that he hoped would convey: "Don't worry, Mom. I *will* be all right! Truly!"

He gave Betty's hand a little squeeze of affection. Married only three months, he was more concerned about being away from her than he was about anything the army or even 'Jerry' might have in store for him. Then his gaze shifted to his silver-haired father whose attempt at assuming an imperative yet unconcerned posture had not fooled him for a second. He knew how much his father loved him.

"Of course, Sir. I'll be fine," Harold answered. "I need only follow your example. You'll watch over Betty for me?"

"Naturally," said his father, smiling at his new daughter-in-law.

Charlie, or more properly Charles Frederick Lawes, had an air of elegance about him. He was attired in a charcoal grey morning coat, a high, stiffly starched white collar, and gun-metal-blue cravat with matching pin-striped trousers, and shiny black leather brogues. His wavy, flowing, silver hair was parted in the middle, and he sported a full handle-bar mustache in the fashion of his older brother, Harry Augustus.

Harry had run away from home, transformed himself into 'Gus Levaine', and made a name for himself on the stages of the London music halls, playing alongside such notables as Charles Coburn, famed for his rendition of "The Man Who Broke the Bank at Monte Carlo." Harry had forever sealed his fate for any hope of returning to the family's bosom when he authored a now infamous song with the rather dubious title, "Sister Mary Walked Like That."

Harry died on May Day in 1936. In August 1939, that seemed a very long time ago. Charlie, the baby of the large family, had not exactly run away from home, but his situation was not unlike that of his older brother. His family had disowned him for marrying Violet. She was Irish and 'beneath his station in life.' Charlie had never really understood those sentiments. After all, his mother, Harriet, had been an orphan when she married his father James in 1853. And James, who had passed away in 1889, had not exactly been a member of the nobility. He had run a 'valentine manufactory' at 242 Albany Road, Camberwell, London, S.E., employing his wife, his six daughters who had survived past childhood – and, of course, Charlie – to illustrate the verses he composed.

Admittedly, Charlie's grandfather, Thomas, had been a man of some means, running stagecoaches between London and Stroud before the railroad came. And James and his older brothers *had* been up to Oxford. Still, by Charlie's standards it was all a bit pretentious.

Charlie had no regrets. He adored his wife who had given him two fine daughters and a strapping son, all of whom showed great promise. What's more, he felt that he and Violet still made one hell of a team. While he, like his sisters, had learned to produce exceptional calligraphy and coloured, hand-painted illustrations, Charlie had always possessed a touch of his older brother's sense of adventure. A superb natural athlete, he had taken to roller-skating, a popular sporting and social activity at the time, when he was in his 20s. It was through roller-skating that he had met Violet, also a devotee.

In May 1898, Charlie had just won first prize at the Lava Rink for backward skating a distance of one mile in 4 minutes 10 seconds when suddenly, he saw her. There, among the boisterous throng anxious to extend their congratulations, stood Violet. Or perhaps stood *out* would be more apt. His eyes found hers and for the rest of the evening he saw no one and nothing else. They were married a few weeks later, and his family cast him out. Undaunted, Charlie and Violet worked up roller skating routines – dances, intricate footwork – hoping to earn their way by performing exhibitions or as instructors of the popular sport and pastime.

At 'Gus Levaine's' suggestion, they developed a routine that could be performed on a theatre stage, the two of them twirling round and round, performing complex manoeuvres and lifts on a raised circular platform a mere 11 feet in diameter. It was not a great success, but it was enough. They were able to keep house and home, begin to raise their first daughter, Irene, born in 1908, and send Charlie back to school to earn his electrical engineering degree.

Lillian arrived in December 1911, only a week after Charlie's certification as an engineer. Harold or 'Toddy' followed – in an unplanned sort of way – five years later. Today, this unintended but most precious son and his lovely new wife were standing before him, unable to contain their youthful buoyancy. Charlie knew better, of course, but he did his best to put on a bold face.

"You just take care of *yourself*, Toddy," he counseled, frowning. "And remember: you were conceived while there was a war going on, and you were born right in the middle of it. You're going to be all right! Your mother and I will look after things here at home."

"And you'll let Rene and Chicks know?" Harold asked, referring to his sisters by their pet names.

Toddy, like his father, was the baby of the family. Albeit theirs was a much smaller family, Toddy loved his sisters dearly. 'Rene' was short for Irene, the oldest of the siblings. She was going to be married in July to a *gentleman,* (the appellation was not accorded lightly) of whom the whole family genuinely approved. More than that, they all liked him, too, for despite his parentage, which could be traced back to English royalty, he was a down-to-earth fellow. William Paar, or Bill as he preferred to be called, held a commission in the Coldstream Guards, and he had already purchased a lovely home for himself and Irene in West Sussex. He, too, had just received his call up notice.

Until a short while ago, Harold had been Irene's accompanist on the piano whenever she sang. Outside of the home, such appearances were normally restricted to weddings, churches, and a select group of upper-crust London supper clubs. He was also invited with increasing regularity to those same clubs to give solo performances.

Indeed the 'in crowd' asserted that Harold Lawes was going to be England's answer to Rachmaninov. He was undeniably a virtuoso at the keyboard and a budding composer, as well. Playing piano, however, was not his normal job. That was with Barclay's Bank where he earned £2.50 a week on the strength of his degree as a Certificated Associate of the Institute of Bankers. But music was in his soul, and he adored the piano. While he was also accomplished on the piano-accordion and the saxophone, he wanted very much to believe what the in crowd kept telling him, (and anyone else who would listen) and quietly harboured aspirations of one day becoming a concert pianist.

'Chicks' was the family nickname for Lillian, Harold's younger sister, a thoroughly modern and strikingly handsome young woman currently involved with a wealthy racing car driver named Kent Jenner who kept a flat in London. She drove almost as fast as he did. A voracious reader, she consumed books of every ilk at a similar pace.

"I won't have time to see either of them before I go back up to camp at Beaulieu," Harold continued, explaining his request. He'd learned excellent Parisian French in school, but, like all his fellow countrymen, he pronounced it *biewlee*.

"Certainly, Toddy," his father assured him. "You will likely get to see Chicks from time to time once you move into the Duke of York's barracks in Chelsea for your training."

Recognizing his patriarch's tone for "dismissed," Harold offered Betty his arm and escorted her out.

As the front door closed, Charlie took Violet in his arms. "Bloody good show, what?" he exclaimed, not certain whether it was his wife or himself that he was trying to reassure.

IN THE DRAWING ROOM, ARMY &
NAVY CLUB, ST. JAMES' SQUARE
September 3, 1939

"Much ado about nothing, if you ask me," said Cecil, his wrinkled cheek pressed up against the window so that he could watch the men piling sand bags around the statue of William III on the bright, sunny morning of September 3, 1939. "It'll all be over in a few weeks."

"What I don't understand," Walter complained in his deep bass voice from his customary high-backed wing chair, "is why the authorities insist on bundling my Charlotte and the grandchildren off to the countryside."

Cecil turned away from his study of the bustling workers and looked over at his oldest, dearest friend. They were the only members in attendance this morning. Well past their prime, the two old veterans of both The Boer War and The Great War spent most of their time at the club these days, drinking tea with biscuits all morning then managing to make a single glass of port last for the entire afternoon. They didn't really come to drink. They came to talk – to reminisce, really – and to enjoy each other's company. But their conversations of late dwelt less on past glories and more on the impending conflict and its implications.

"They took Farquharson, too," Cecil told his friend, returning to his seat across from Walter. "It's not just pregnant women and children, you know. It's the invalids and the handicapped, as well. All being taken to the countryside. It's the planes they're worried about. Dropping bombs, you know."

People who didn't know him would look at Cecil and see a frail, well-used old man. In truth, he was still very fit and wiry for his 73 years. There was still a spark of defiant energy burning brightly inside, and it shone in his eyes.

Walter, by contrast, would rightly be judged somewhat overweight, sedentary, and even lethargic. He had always been rather stout, but now, as he neared his 75th birthday, his girth was threatening to force him out of his favourite chair and onto the sofa.

"Well, we know about that, don't we?" Walter rumbled. "Blighters couldn't hit a football field from 500 feet up! Plenty of noise to be sure, but no real harm done… Hmn?"

"You read in the papers what they did in Poland," Cecil gently reminded his friend. "These aeroplanes are much bigger than what they had in our time. They no longer hold the bombs over the side of the things and drop them by hand, you know. They open a door in the belly of the plane and drop *dozens* of bombs, all at once!"

"And what's all this nonsense," Walter continued his harangue, as if Cecil hadn't spoken a word, "about 'blacking out' our windows at night? Hmn? What's the point of having scrimped all these years to retire in comfort in a nice house in a nice neighbourhood with nice scenery to look at outside my parlor window? Hmn?"

At that moment, the club steward, Stilson, rushed, breathless into the drawing room—a most uncharacteristic display of energy for a man who was older than either of the members present.

"Excuse me, gentlemen," he panted, going straight to the sideboard and switching on the wireless. Walter glared at the man for the full 40 seconds it took for the radio to warm up. Stilson fiddled with the tuning knob, then increased the volume.

"This morning," Prime Minister Neville Chamberlain's thin, reedy voice came over the airwaves, *"the British Ambassador in Berlin handed the German government a final note stating that unless the British government heard by 11 o'clock that they were prepared to withdraw their troops from Poland, a state of war would exist between us. I have to tell you now that no such undertaking has been received and that, consequently, this country is at war with Germany... it is evil things that we shall be fighting against— brute force, bad faith, injustice, suppression, and persecution, and against them I am certain that the right will prevail."*

Stilson turned off the machine. Cecil and Walter looked at one another in silence for several heartbeats.

"Bloody right!" Cecil finally broke the tension. "Now they're for it!" His eyes sparkled with an intensity that his friend had not seen in them for many years.

"Bloody right!" echoed Walter. "Blighters should have known better than to rouse the English lion! They'll soon enough rue the day!"

"Well done, Mr. Stilson," Cecil commended the steward, who was still standing at the radio on the sideboard. "I believe under the circumstances it would not be inappropriate if we were to take our port a little earlier than usual today. And perhaps, Mr. Stilson..." Cecil glanced over at his friend.

"... you would care to join us," Walter finished for him.

Charlie & Toddy

The Lawes Family 1939

2

BRITAIN

Fall 1939 through Spring 1940

Every man on the parade square was convinced that the Sergeant's voice, his word of command, could not possibly be human in origin. It seemed to come up from the tarmac through the soles of his boots, issue from what must surely be a painfully distended jaw... and then somehow find its way to every nerve-ending in a man's body.

"Tallest on the left, shortest on the right. In three ranks. Size!"

(*Here now, what's all this pushing and shoving then?* Harold wondered.)

"Open orderrr... march! Ri-i-ight... dress! Le-e-eft... turn! By the left, qui-i-ick... march! Ri-i-ight... wheel! Companyyy... halt! Ri-i-ight—*wait for it...* turn! Slo-o-ope... arms!"

(*On and on, around and around the parade square at the prescribed regulation 120 paces per minute until the Company Sergeant Major was satisfied... which seemed to be a rare event, indeed!*)

"You dozy little man! You 'orrible creature! Polish those buttons! Shine those boots! You call that a regulation knot?

(*Just how much* was *the Sergeant's idea of a little spit and polish?*)

"What does WWCP stand for? Cretin! Look it up! Next man... What do you mean, what *is* an UXB? You're a proper case, aren't you, Wilkins?"

(*Why does the military have to have an abbreviation or an acronym for everything and everyone?* Harold wondered again. *And while we're at it, what is the point of being able to bounce a shilling dropped from shoulder height off the top sheet of your cot?*)

"Slo-o-ow... march! Ey-y-yes... right! Pree-zent... arms!"

(*Are they training us to fight a war? Or for a ceremonial march-past in front of His Majesty? We're sure as hell not likely to do any 'slo-o-ow' bloody marching over there!*)

"Squad will fix bayonets. Fi-i-ix bay'nets!"

(*I'll fix you, Corporal, you dirty little…*)

"Stand a-a-at... ease! Stand easy, men! Smoke if you 'ave 'em."

(*Couldn't we sit down, just for a few minutes?*)

"Move to the right in column of route. Ri-i-ight... turn! Qui-i-ick... march! March easy, men!"

(*Here we are in full service marching order—Lee Enfield rifle, small pack, and gas mask, large pack on back, tin hat and gas cape strapped to large pack, water bottle on hip, regulation amount of ammunition... He must think he's Stanley Holloway!* Harold mused to himself.)

In the early going, Harold's self-confidence proved to be well founded. Basic training proceeded on schedule. Not once was he the object of, "Corporal, take that man's name!" and, most importantly, he was able to get away on leave frequently to see Betty and his parents and sisters, despite being moved about the country every few months. Betty found a clerical position with the War Department, and young Harold was proud that his wife was going to be 'doing her bit.'

While billeted at the White House in Bolcombe in November, he was promoted to Lance Corporal and presumed that this meant he would soon see action. After all, the British Expeditionary Force was already over in France just waiting for a chance to have at the Germans. Admittedly, nothing much appeared to be happening in France just now, but surely, he and his fellows would be needed there soon.

Discouragingly, he was wrong. The next four months were spent at Brighton, taking a few turns at manning the anti-aircraft guns and eventually becoming acclimatized to the horrendous racket they produced; driving on roads that boasted even more and bigger craters than London's own; and learning how to move petrol and other supplies by various and devious means while supposedly 'under fire.'

Predictably, the weather was cold, wet, and generally miserable. But the food was surprisingly good, even by army standards. Rationing had not yet become as severe as it would in the near future. And, the company was especially good by any standards. It seemed to Harold that the RASC had managed to attract – or conscript – men from all walks of life, and he soon discovered, somewhat to his own surprise, that he got along well with virtually all of them, from dustman to gentleman. It helped, of course, that he had known more than a few of his mates in private life before the war had thrust them all together with a collection of perfect strangers. But former friend or new acquaintance, it seemed they all shared much in common: not least their love of King and country, their shared conviction of being in the right, and their irrepressible confidence in both themselves and in one another.

That such a large group of men from such diverse backgrounds could have so quickly and completely coalesced into a well-coordinated unit was astounding to some, while others seemed to take it for granted. Whatever one's individual perspective on the matter, all soon learned to take pride in their collective efforts, particularly when it became clear that those efforts were paying off. As the days went by not only were the instructors finding fewer and fewer reasons for criticizing or correcting, but they also actually seemed to be easing up on their normal demands. And despite the inclement weather, Brighton was still Brighton. It was almost like being on holiday if one overlooked barrage balloons... which struck him as being woefully ineffectual against the occasional air raid.

Harold found that he enjoyed the ready camaraderie, the physical demands of the training, and the opportunity to acquire new technical skills. For any man in his early 20s, much of the training was exciting and even seemed somehow glamourous at times. If one imagined himself being watched by others, (civilians, not the Corporal or the Sergeant!) while tearing down a country road between the hedgerows at full clip behind the wheel of a monstrous lorry... or charging across a field with fixed bayonet, for example... why, it was almost like being in the movies.

On the other hand, there were always the decidedly *un*glamorous activities, like polishing your brass or washing the lorries or digging latrine trenches.

He learned how to identify dozens of different airplanes, both friendly and hostile, by their silhouettes viewed from various angles. He qualified as an expert marksman with the .303 Lee Enfield rifle. He mastered the grenade launcher, the anti-tank rifle, the sten gun, the bren gun, and the Thompson submachine gun. The Lewis and Hotchkiss machine guns were leftovers from his father's war, but thanks to Charlie's supplemental tutelage he could soon strip and reassemble either one even faster than his instructors. And he had inherited Charlie's athletic physique and stamina.

On the parade square, despite being of average height and build, he stood out because his every movement was crisp and precise. On cross-country route marches, in full kit and carrying a rifle, he never flagged, even on the hottest days. On the obstacle courses, he always finished among the leaders. He bested the chief instructor in unarmed combat two falls out of three, five times out of five. He could lob a grenade as far and as accurately as the two professional cricket bowlers in the unit. He learned how to drive and how to maintain vehicles of every shape and size: motorcycles, vans, fifteen-hundred weights, three-tonne lorries, armoured personnel carriers, tankers, tanks, and tank-transporters.

In some ways it was like being back at school, and Harold found the challenge and the competition exhilarating. He was popular in turn for his enthusiasm, ready wit, good humour, and of course, his musical talents, especially his piano playing. Added to his extensive pre-war repertoire were such popular tunes of the day as, "Lillie Marlene," "Bless 'em All," and "We're Going To Hang Out the Washing on the Siegfired Line!" Once his virtuosity on the piano became generally known, he was often prevailed upon to play at impromptu parties, not only by his own unit but by others, as well. And there were many, many parties during these troubled times, as people from all walks of life sought every opportunity to alleviate the pervading sense of doom and gloom.

Yet, as the weeks crept by there was a sense of unreality, as well. The long-anticipated clouds of massed German bombers over southern England had so far failed to materialize. Whatever action was taking place seemed somehow remote and impersonal, and the headlines on the front pages of the newspapers might almost be viewed as isolated events rather than parts of a coordinated war effort. Still, you had to believe that there was some organizing going on somewhere. Every day there was more evidence of that.

Now, for example, there were Canadian troops and even a few Australian airmen mingling with the locals on the dance floors. Huge silver barrage balloons could be seen floating above all the major cities. Little corrugated Anderson shelters were springing up in backyards everywhere. Rationing had finally begun in earnest, targeting butter, sugar, and bacon, and rumour said it would soon include all meat.

Caught up as they were in all the training and all the learning and all the parties, Harold and the other members of his outfit had rarely succumbed to the tantalizing wiles of rumour. Rather, their most persistent temptress was cloaked in a different if no less seductive veil. The promise of action. They were all growing impatient. There was fighting going on and they wanted to be a part of it.

Harold's youthful self-confidence, far from having been in any way diminished, was in fact buoyant. Hadn't he, had not *all* of them, acquired so much new, valuable knowledge, so many new, practical skills? They were ready. If anything, he felt... no, he *knew* without doubt, that he and his mates were more than ready for whatever 'Jerry' might have in store for them.

IN THE DRAWING ROOM
May 13, 1940

"Inspirational!" proclaimed Cecil, rather loudly. He took a larger than usual sip of his port. "Yes, that's the word I was searching for. Inspirational!"

A number of the 30 or so members in the drawing room, most in uniform, looked over at Cecil and nodded or raised a glass to him to signify their agreement.

"Hmn?" growled Walter. "Churchill offers us nothing but 'blood, toil, tears, and sweat' and you find that *inspirational*?"

"Oh, come now, Walter," said Cecil, lowering his voice and attempting to mollify his friend. "Even *you* must admit that his speech was quite stirring, you know. Didn't it get the old ticker pumping just a little bit faster?"

"No, Sir! He's just another bloody politician, no better or worse than Chamberlain before him. They can make all the speeches they want to from here to Doomsday and I'll not be roused by their vacuous words."

Walter put his hand on the arm of his chair and leaned forward, eyes narrowing, fixing Cecil with a stern look.

"It's *action*, Sir... action, I say, that stirs my blood. Like the gallant deeds of the lads of the *HMS Cossack* when they rescued 300 of our prisoners of war from that German ship in a Norwegian fjord back in February." Nodding in approval of his own observation, he slowly sat back in his big wing chair. "Now *that*," he pontificated, "was truly inspirational! Hmn?"

"But Walter, at the time..." Cecil hesitated, looking down at his hands clasped in his lap. "At the time you said it was a... a 'political blunder of the first magnitude' were your exact words, I believe. You insisted that it would bring neutral Norway into the war... against us."

"Now, Cecil," Walter protested. "Don't you try to steer the conversation back to politics. I'm trying to respond to your question about what it is that gets my blood up. Hmn?"

"But Walter, I was only..."

"I'll give you another fine example!" Walter pushed on, crossing his legs and stretching them out as he eased his bulk forward in his increasingly confining chair. "'Twas the Senior Service again, bless 'em. Only ones who can do anything right in this cursed affair!"

"Walter," Cecil interjected almost timorously, "if you mean to revisit the encounter of the British flotilla with the enemy fleet at Narvik last month, well then, I do hope..."

"Precisely, old man!" Walter beamed, bolting into as upright a position as his considerable frame allowed. "Nine, *nine,* need I remind you, of the enemy's puissant destroyers sunk by England's incomparable Royal Navy over the course of only two days!" Walter sat back again, steepling his fingers in front of his face and looking at his friend with an accusatory expression, as if challenging Cecil to rebut the probity of his example.

Cecil had endured just about enough of Walter's selective memory. He drained his glass of port and much more shockingly – whether to his long-time friend or to Mr. Stilson, it was unclear – signaled for two more glasses of the sweet, fortified wine.

Head slightly bowed, his eyes shifting in slow, measured beats from his friend's face to his own knees to a spot far off in space, Cecil remained silent until Stilson had placed the two fresh glasses of port wine on the small table between them and discreetly withdrawn.

"No, thank you, Walter. You have no need to remind me of any detail concerning that illustrious event." He spoke quietly yet the timbre of his voice now possessed an inexplicable authority that made the larger man – Walter's first glass of port was still only half consumed – hold his silence.

"Rather, I was about to remind *you.*" Cecil's normal undulating tenor assumed the professional monotone of a BBC broadcaster. "I was about to remind *you* of what you said—rather loudly, so as to ensure that the other dozen or so club members present at the time, when the news came over the wireless would be sure to hear." Cecil could no longer look at his friend. "You said, Walter, and I quote: 'Even the bleeding politicians can't ask us to swallow that one! *Nine* of the enemy's great destroyers? I suppose next they'll expect us to believe that Nelson has come back from the dead!'"

"Well now, I... huhmn! I ah... I do recall making some reference to Lord Nelson," Walter mumbled, looking at his toes.

"You can't continue having it both ways, Walter," Cecil instructed. "You can't go on loudly criticizing everyone and everything one moment then quietly and privately changing your tune, as it suits you, the next. I won't have it."

A deep salmon colour rose swiftly from Walter's collar, like the mercury of a thermometer plunged into boiling water, and bright pink splotches appeared on his cheeks and forehead. "Now look here, Sir!" he blustered, bracing himself to rise.

"I'm not finished, Walter," Cecil continued calmly. The big man reluctantly settled back in his chair.

"You and I go back a long way, Walter. *I* know how fiercely patriotic you are and that you are no less genuinely proud of our men in uniform, whatever the service, than I. But some of these lads," he went on, his eyes slowly sweeping the drawing room, "know only that you are a highly decorated former naval officer. Many of them, especially the younger ones who have not yet been blooded, take one look at that conspicuous gallantry medal ribbon on your chest and, even without knowing how you earned it, immediately class you as someone to be respected. Indeed, their respect borders on awe. They hang on your every word, you know."

All the time he was speaking Cecil had been regarding his old friend closely, trying to judge whether his message was getting through. Walter, his colour slowly returning to normal, picked up his half-finished first glass of port and raised it in salute.

"Quite right, old man," he murmured contritely. He looked into the unblinking eyes boring into him from across the little table, smiled broadly, and took a deep breath. In a steadier voice he said simply: "Thank you, Cecil, my friend!" Walter gulped the remains of the first glass and, wiping at a tear, picked up the second.

3

BRITAIN

June through November 1940

A new word for a new kind of war: *Blitzkrieg!* Denmark, the Netherlands, Belgium, Luxembourg, France: one after one, the countries of northern continental Europe had been overrun by the seemingly ineluctable juggernaut that was the Third Reich's war machine.

Early in June 1940, almost 11 months following his call up and with Churchill's "We shall fight them on the beaches" still ringing in his ears, Harold was promoted to full Corporal. Billeted at Maidstone, he persuaded the Regimental Sergeant Major to let him drive around to his parents' house on a Matchless motorcycle, where he proudly showed off the second stripe on his new battle jacket—a short, woolen thing with tightly fitting waist and cuffs. It was good to be based close to home again. It allowed him to see Betty and his family much more frequently.

"This is brilliant, Mom," Harold enthused, piercing another tiny morsel of the succulent rutabaga with his fork. "I don't know how you do it!"

He ate at his parents' house whenever the opportunity presented itself. Violet was a very good cook and had a flare for enhancing even the simplest ingredients with a pinch of this, a *soupçon* of that, and a lot of imagination. With rationing now so stringent – two ounces of tea per person per week and only one egg per person per week, for example – a home-cooked meal supplemented by vegetables and herbs from the family garden was truly something to savour. Barracks fare, regardless of the advertised ingredients, all tended to taste pretty much the same, and Betty's cooking… well, Betty didn't exhibit much talent in the kitchen. No matter how many extra ration coupons Harold managed to scrounge for her, she never seemed to be able to cobble together what could honestly be called a decent supper.

"It gladdens my heart to know that you still enjoy my cooking, Toddy," Violet smiled. "If you, and Betty, of course," she added deferentially, "can come 'round Friday, I should have a bit of meat. Or if not then fish perhaps. I'll talk to Rene and see if she might come up to join us."

"If it's to be a family gathering," said Charlie from behind his newspaper, "why don't you three girls pool the meat coupons you saved from last week with this week's and I'll see if I can't persuade the butcher to let us have a proper joint of beef. Should be able to procure a leg of mutton at the very least."

"What a splendid idea, Charlie!" his wife beamed. She looked over at Betty.

"I, uh…" Betty blushed, lowering her eyes to her empty plate. "I'm afraid I've used mine."

Twisting the napkin in her lap, keeping her head bowed, she raised her eyes briefly and glanced nervously across the table at Harold whose face at that moment was the personification of incredulity.

"Surely, you don't mean this week's as well as last!" he said rather louder than he intended, unable to bridle his exasperation. He had not taken a meal in the little flat that he and Betty called home in over a month, and he had been providing her with extra ration coupons all that time. Her head bowed even lower, but she didn't offer any response. He sat there contemplating the top of Betty's head for a moment until Charlie peered at him over the top of his newspaper. He tried to look his father straight in the eye but, unable to find any words adequate to the situation, he was forced to look down at his own dinner plate. It was Harold's turn to blush.

———— ❦ ————

Later that evening, when the children had left – Harold back to his barracks and Betty to their little flat – Violet and Charlie were alone in their big kitchen doing the dishes. She washed and Charlie dried. It was a familiar and comfortable routine, usually accompanied by idle, mostly pointless chatter or a review of the day's news reports. The previous evening, for example, they had commiserated with one another over Italy's entrance into the war—an ally in World War I now declaring for 'The Bosch,' as Charlie still called the Germans. Today's headlines had contained nothing so momentous to fuel their conversation and besides, this evening neither of them felt inclined to be the first to break the silence.

Even after Chicks and Rene had moved out, the big old rambling house had not begun to feel too large for their needs. The girls and their gentlemen friends had been frequent visitors before the war broke out. Now, though, with Rene's Bill posted to Malta and so much of Chicks' time being taken up driving ambulances or transport trucks for the Home Guard, such visits were less and less common. Toddy, of course, had moved out shortly after his marriage to Betty. In retrospect, that had been only a few weeks before his call up. Since then, what with all the excitement, there had been no time to reflect on how empty the place now felt.

The unnatural silence between them was becoming oppressive. Unconsciously, Charlie started applying more and more vigour to his dish-drying chores, so much so that suddenly the crystal glass in his hands broke, inflicting a small cut between thumb and forefinger.

"Blast!" he cursed, one of the strongest profanities to have escaped his lips since returning to civilian life back in 1919. ('Bloody,' a word which he and so many other Englishmen, genteel or otherwise, almost invariably found the opportunity to employ several times a day, did not qualify as an expletive, in Charlie's opinion. Rather, it was simply a good old all-purpose English adjective, perfectly acceptable on any occasion—even in mixed company.)

"Sorry, my love," he offered contritely, sucking on the wound. "That was one of the good ones, too."

"Here, let me look at it," Violet demanded solicitously, pulling his hand away from his mouth. "Nothing serious," she pronounced. "I'll just fetch some disinfectant."

As Violet ran off to the medicine chest Charlie slumped down at the kitchen table and resumed his sucking. As soon as she returned, he proffered his hand for her ministrations and looked at her tenderly.

"She's still very young," he said. "I need to keep reminding myself."

"Yes, dear," Violet acknowledged, scarcely looking up from the focus of her attention.

"And with Toddy being away so much so soon after the wedding... it must be very difficult for her."

When Violet remained quiet, he withdrew his injured hand obliging her to look up at him. "Wouldn't you agree?" he asked, frowning.

"Yes, dear," his wife conceded, reaching for his hand again. "It's just that sometimes, like this evening... I can't help wondering if..."

Finally, Violet relented. Releasing Charlie's hand, she sat back and crossed her arms under her bosom. "What's done is done, me lad. Spilt milk an' all." She tried to keep her voice firm and resolute, but it was no use pretending any longer. "And while it is unfortunate, I must agree with your assessment of our daughter-in-law," she sniffled.

"Only 21, a tender age," Charlie started to embellish.

"No, not that," Violet interrupted him. "That's not what I meant at all. I know that's what you were saying, but what I meant was that I agree with what you're *not* saying."

The downcast look on Charlie's face told that he knew what was coming. He leaned forward and gently placed a hand on Violet's knee. "And what precisely is it that I am *not* saying?"

She looked directly at him then, not allowing her gaze to waver though her eyes brimmed with tears. It was a look that defied him to disagree with her. "Our Toddy deserves better and we both know it."

Now his training was as a dispatch rider and motorized convoy escort. In this capacity, for the very first time, Harold was permitted to carry a side arm rather than a .303 rifle. He spent as many hours as he could – legitimately or through finagling – on the firing range with his new 'toy', a .45 revolver. The finagled times allowed him to experiment with some techniques that were not strictly speaking by the book. More importantly, as subsequent events were to unfold, at such times there were almost always a few old hands on site who were more than willing to share the tricks of the trade with an obviously keen youngster who demonstrated a flare for the use of a handgun.

Over the next four months, Harold managed to see from the back of a motorcycle more of the English countryside – not to mention parts of Wales and Scotland – than he had ever hoped or intended.

Adventure, of course, is seldom without incident. Among the most memorable occurred on July 10th. As part of a routine training exercise – 'play acting' they called it – he was part of a supposed advance reconnaissance team out of Cardiff towards Bridgend in southern Wales when the Germans decided, for reasons known only to themselves, finally to launch the first phase of what would soon become known as the Battle of Britain. In short, the *Luftwaffe* chose that particular day to launch a massive bombing raid on the docks in south Wales. (The same day they also went after, in strength, a convoy of coasters steaming west from Dover to Dungeness, but Harold didn't even hear about that attack until two days later.) Straddling his motorcycle at the top of a hill, Harold watched the explosions from several kilometres away. It turned out to be a safe distance for him, but two other members of the squad who were play acting at reconnaissance were killed and one other severely injured in the unexpectedly large bombing raid.

For the next few weeks, the long-anticipated and much dreaded flights of German bombers filled the skies at all hours of the day and night, targeting shipping and harbours. France had capitulated and the new Vichy government had officially severed relations with Britain. The Soviet Union was taking full advantage of the disarray the Germans were causing in Europe: Lithuania, Latvia, Estonia, and incursions into Romania. Italy was flexing its muscles in British Somaliland and even Egypt. German U-boats were boasting of 'Happy Days' in their efforts to isolate Britain by sinking hundreds of merchant ships attempting to cross the Atlantic in convoys bearing desperately needed supplies from the New World. Half-way around the world Japan's new militaristic leadership was making outrageous territorial demands, most of which were being conceded with little or no meaningful objection from the European powers.

The Battle of Britain raged at unprecedented levels and in August the *Luftwaffe* shifted their primary targets from shipping to airfields and to major industrial cities. Central London itself had been bombed. Although it would be some time before the profoundly apt epithet became a standard reference point in any subsequent discussion of the war, The London Blitz was well and truly underway.

Harold feared for Betty's safety and for the safety of his parents and his sisters, but he felt helpless to do anything about it. As if the authorities were oblivious to the horrible realities inundating their tiny island – and it was painfully clear now that Britain stood alone against the Axis powers with only her loyal commonwealth members for support – for him the never-ending training dragged on and on. Oh, there was still much that was new and interesting, occasionally even challenging. But inevitably his thoughts returned to one inescapable theme. Was it all meaningless? Was it hopeless? In the name of all that's sacred, *"When are they going to let us fight?"*

In November he was promoted to Sergeant. Some anonymous clerk in the Records Office had evidently unearthed commendations on his parade-square 'smartness' ratings from base camp on the basis of which an equally anonymous superior had determined that Sergeant Lawes would be ideally suited to serve the RASC as a drill instructor. A six-week training course with the King's Own ensued where among other esoteric niceties he learned how to march precisely.

This involved the use of a split or divided baton resembling a geometric compass and called, officially, a 'drill stick.' Hinged at the top, each leg of this ingenious device sprouted three inches of pointed steel at the bottom. Spread to the maximum angle permitted by the hinge, the distance between the steel points measured exactly 30 inches. The idea was, holding the top or hinged end of the compass lightly in the right hand, to set the tip of one leg on the ground next to the right heel with the end of the other leg slightly off the ground and pointed down the line of march.

"By the left," the instructor spoke in an almost conversational tone, "take one step forward, but leave your right foot flat on the ground. Now set the second leg of the drill stick on the ground parallel to the line of march. If your left heel is now the same distance from your right heel as the forward point of the drill stick is from the back one, then you have taken a correct marching stride. Raise the back leg of the drill stick. Keeping your left foot flat on the ground step forward with the right foot. As you are stepping use the forward point of the drill stick as a pivot and twirl the back leg *away* from you through 180 degrees so that it becomes the forward leg, pointed down the line of march and set the tip on the ground. If your right heel is exactly beside the point of the drill stick, which is now in the forward position, then you have taken a correct marching stride. Got the idea now, Sergeant Lawes? Simple enough, what?"

"Er, yes, Sir," Harold answered uncertainly.

"Right then. I'll leave you to practise on you own. When you can go twice 'round the parade square at a forced-march rate of 160 paces per minute without dropping the drill stick and without taking an incorrect marching stride you will be ready for the next lesson. Come and find me."

It was fully two weeks before Sergeant Lawes went looking for the soft-spoken instructor and not without considerable trepidation as to what the next lesson might entail. At the end of the six-week course he returned to his own unit where he was accorded the rank of Sergeant Major Instructor and placed in charge of training in drill, small arms and unarmed combat, with a commensurate rise in pay. In this new capacity he dutifully served for the next five months. Dutifully, but not happily.

Now in the army there are instructors and there are Instructors. Any Lance Corporal put in charge of a squad could legitimately be called an instructor. But if one's official rank included the designation Instructor – with a capital 'I' – well, these individuals were looked upon as a breed apart. In most cases they were chosen for their positions for the obvious reason that they were very good, personally, at whatever subject or activity they were assigned to teach. Indeed, it was generally conceded that they were better at whatever their specialty or specialties might be than the rank and file whom they were charged with upgrading. A qualified Instructor was a respected, highly valued member of the military establishment. All of this was well and good, Harold repeatedly told himself. There was just one catch: Thinking back over the 15 months since he had been called to the colours, Harold recalled the name of every one of the Instructors who had at one point or another had him under their charge. He knew only too well that every one of them was to this day still in the same place they had been when he had first encountered them.

In the British army, Instructors instructed. They did not go into battle. They were not posted to operational units. They certainly never set foot on hostile ground. Precisely because they were deemed to be so valuable doing what they were doing where they were doing it, Instructors tended to be kept where they were. And now Harold was one of them. He supposed he should feel some pride in having achieved this distinction, but the prospect of having the war pass him by without seeing any action was dismaying.

IN THE DRAWING ROOM
August 22, 1940

"You're right again, Cecil. The man undeniably has a way with words," Walter conceded grudgingly.

"More tea, old chap?" asked Cecil, offering to pour. When Walter nodded, he generously tipped the remaining contents of the pot into his friend's cup. "I'm afraid that's the last of it."

Walter hardly noticed. He had closed his eyes, trying to remember Churchill's latest speech word for word. "How did it go again? "Never in the field of human conflict..." he began quoting.

"Inspirational?" Cecil teased, one thin, white eyebrow arched high.

The big man opened his eyes, uttered a short barking sound, something between a grunt and a laugh, and sat forward reaching for his tea. "You'll not let me off the hook, will you?"

"Just tuggin' yer trews, you know," Cecil smiled.

Walter shook his head slowly from side to side. The admiration in his regard was patently unreserved. "I still marvel at your resilience, even after all these years and all we've been through together," he said earnestly. "I've never met another who could measure up to you when it comes to pure strength of character."

"Don't get maudlin on me, old chap. There's no call for that," said Cecil, blushing slightly, despite himself.

"But... how can you sit here, smiling and cracking lame jokes? You've lost *everything,* Cecil! It was a direct hit!"

Walter's tone held an almost pleading quality for it was truly incomprehensible to him how any man – even Cecil – could present such an outwardly cheerful countenance on the morning after his house and all his worldly goods, had been reduced to ashes by an incendiary bomb.

"Oh, but you're wrong, you know. You're wrong, Walter," Cecil asserted. "Indeed, I consider myself a very fortunate man. Why, as things stand I must be one of the very few Londoners who has not had to mourn the loss of a family member or a friend or even had to worry about the implications of some serious injury to one of them. Which reminds me,

Walter, that young nephew of yours... have you heard...?" Cecil's voice trailed off at the grimace of pain that contorted his friend's face.

After a long pause punctuated by a deep, resigned sigh Walter was able find his voice. "He'll never realize his life-long dream of becoming a professional footballer but... the doctors hold out hope that given time he may be able to walk again with some sort of metal brace fitted over." He coughed trying to clear his throat. "Fitted over what's left of his knee."

"I'm so sorry, Walter," said Cecil, standing and laying a comforting hand on his friend's shoulder.

"Yes, well," Walter managed after another deep-seated cough. "As you say, my friend, we must all learn to be thankful for small mercies."

April 1939 - Joins Territorial Army

Driver Lawes, RASC

May 1940 - Lance Corporal

June 1940 - Full Corporal

November 1940 - Sergeant

4

BOSCOMBE, SOUTH COAST OF ENGLAND
January through February 1941

It might have been the same anonymous clerk in the Records Office who had albeit indirectly been responsible for Sergeant Lawes' transformation into a Sergeant Major Instructor. It might have been the same anonymous senior who once again endorsed the recommendation. Harold never did find out. Nevertheless, evidently someone, somewhere, had taken the trouble to look not only at his Record of Service since he had joined the RASC, but also beyond at his academic record and professional training in civilian life. To anyone seeing the two in concert his qualifications as a candidate were obvious. Or perhaps it was simply that the Service Corps had another need—one that exceeded their need for instructors.

In January 1941, Harold was sent down to the Officer Cadet Training Unit (OCTU) at Boscombe on the Channel coast. There he studied such varied subjects as: "Intelligence, Information and Security," "Discipline, Office Work and Burial Parties," "Supply and Replenishment of Material in the Field," "Field Engineering," "Mechanized Movement by Road," and others ranging from map reading to signals. And he became the best shot with a handgun that any of the OCTU training staff could ever recall having seen.

"Remarkable! Absolutely remarkable!" the Commandant said aloud to no one in particular as he watched Cadet Lawes going through his paces on the firing range.

It didn't seem to matter whether he was firing a standard issue .45 revolver or one of the ubiquitous Colt .45 automatic pistols that in seemingly unlimited numbers they had been able to purchase from the United States. He was deadly accurate, and he was incredibly fast. It was not the unerring sequence of bullseyes that Harold scored from the prone, kneeling, and standing positions that evoked the Commandant's soliloquy. Rather it was the evidence of his prowess after the command for "rapid fire!" had been given. The bullseye of Harold's target had been obliterated before most of the other soldiers on the line had triggered off their third shots from their six shot revolvers.

"Absolutely remarkable!" the Commandant repeated himself.

"I couldn't agree more, Sir," murmured a surprisingly young-looking visiting Major, standing to the Commandant's left. He took a pace back and turned toward the Commandant's Adjutant, who stood to the Colonel's right.

"Tell me about this man," he said quietly.

The Adjutant was also a Major and arguably the senior of the two, having served in World War I. Yet, there was no mistaking the tone of voice. That "tell me" was not a polite request but rather, an order.

The younger man was an official observer from a mysterious Special Operations unit, and he was known to be travelling about the country visiting most if not all the units in training. His reputation had preceded him, so he was not entirely welcome. It was a widely known and much resented fact among Commanding officers (CO) in virtually every branch of the service that this interloping Major was, for all intents and purposes, recruiting a private army—an army comprised exclusively of all the very best men to be found anywhere in uniform. Understandably, COs were loath to lose men whom they had trained and nurtured for months to *make* them the best. The damnable thing about it was, the orders from on high were very clear: this Major was not to be questioned, challenged, or denied. Although no one would confirm it, his authority was said to come directly from number 10 Downing Street.

Reddening a little, the Adjutant swallowed the resentment he felt at being addressed by the younger officer in such a manner and harrumphed that he was not personally acquainted with every man serving under the King's colours.

"Perhaps you could arrange for me to speak with his instructors," suggested the Special Ops man, not willing to be put off. This was as close as he would come to phrasing his order deferentially.

The requested meetings were arranged that very afternoon. When they were concluded, the Major from Special Operations spent half an hour closeted with the Commandant in the latter's office. Several telephone calls were made. Then the Major departed without another word to anyone.

Harold was totally unaware that any of these events, wherein he had been the focus of attention, had transpired.

At the end of February, Harold emerged from OCTU with the single pips and Sam Browne of a Second Lieutenant.

Harold had been asked by the Commandant to play the piano during the meal at the formal graduation ceremony of the newly promoted officers in the Chine Hotel, and he readily agreed. He spent two hours putting together a program of light classics, which he decided would provide an unobtrusive background to the meal and to the conversations of the diners.

There were a number of civilian guests, among them and seated at the place of honour on the Colonel's right, was Vera Lynn, Britain's most popular songstress of the time. To her right sat Charlie Kunz, "The Piano Medley King," with whose band Miss Lynn had long been associated. Both were well-known celebrities, and both were respected, not only for their talents, but also for their contributions to the morale of the enlisted men and women through their free concerts. That indeed was the reason for their presence this very evening. They had volunteered to entertain the graduating officers after dinner.

Events did not transpire quite as had been anticipated.

The remains of the roast beef and Yorkshire pudding had been cleared and the *crème brulée* dessert was being served with a choice (at the head table only) of brandy or port. The Commandant turned to Mr. Kunz and England's favourite songstress and diffidently suggested, "Perhaps, when you have finished your port and your brandy, Miss Lynn, Mr. Kunz... we could impose upon the two of you..."

Charlie Kunz, acknowledged by many as the most popular recording artist of his day, froze the Commandant with a look that spoke volumes. "Of course, Colonel. *We* would be delighted. But frankly, you needn't have bothered asking *me* to come," Charlie opined, glancing at Vera with an expression on his face that she had never seen before. Charlie Kunz had grown up in the United States, but he affected an accent that made him sound like Ronald Coleman whom he fancied he resembled. He looked over to Vera again as if for approval. Her eyelids slowly closed in acknowledgment – and agreement – of what she thought he was about to say. A polite, generous complement from the professional for the efforts of the young amateur at the piano. (He *was* rather good!)

"I beg your pardon, I mean, really, I..." the Colonel blustered. "Why on earth not?" he finally managed.

"Because, Sir," Charlie stated with diffidence, "you already have a man sitting at the piano who is a finer pianist than I shall ever be."

He looked at Vera as if expecting her to protest his assertion. When she did not, he refocused on his host, swallowed, and startled even himself by saying: "You know, Colonel, you really shouldn't be sending that young man into a theatre of war. Oh, he belongs on the stage... of the Albert Hall!"

The Colonel's look of utter stupefaction stretched to a full three seconds.

"You don't say!" he protested. While trying desperately to decide whether he was being put upon by the famous artist, he looked over in the direction of his newly commissioned subaltern (*What was his name again? Ah, yes, Cadet... no, no,* Lieutenant *Lawes.*) For a few moments, indeed, for the first time that evening, he actually listened to the playing.

"Mmmm," he pursed his lips. "Mm-hmm. Not too bad," he allowed, just volubly enough that Charlie and Vera could hear him, all the while nodding his head to demonstrate beyond question his acquiescence with the bandleader's assessment (and all the while silently reminding himself: *'You're tone deaf, you old sot!'*) "Not bad at all."

While the Colonel's music appreciation skills were perhaps under-developed, his appreciation of all things military and, particularly, anything to do with his present command was arguably over-developed. And this was one of his men that "The King of the Piano Melody" ... or, "The Piano's Melody King"... or ... No matter! This renowned celebrity sitting beside him had said that the man was good. One of *his* men. No, correct that. One of his finest.

"Well, er, now that you mention it, of course I, um, I personally selected Lieutenant Lawes to provide our, um, the, er, divertissement during this evening's meal," the Colonel preened, confident that his distinguished guests would be impressed with his worldliness. "It was not an easy choice by any means. Oh no, not by a long shot. Why, we are blessed with so many talented musicians, dancers, footballers, cricketers, and... and, I dare say, even opera singers among our current collection of young men!"

Recognizing from the expressions on the faces of the two celebrity guests that he was stretching the point beyond credulity he lifted his napkin, ostensibly to wipe his lips, giving himself time to collect his thoughts. "But as you say, Mr. Kunz, this one has a certain, ah, shall we say, a certain *je ne sais quoi*. Yes? I'm sure you agree." He actually batted his eyelashes a few times at Charlie Kunz before remembering himself and redirecting his fluttering lids to Vera Lynn.

Charlie and Vera looked at one another and managed with laudable self-control to refrain from bursting into laughter at the ebullient pomposity that the Colonel had mustered in a vain attempt to conceal his discomfiture. As Charlie was turning back to the Colonel to respond, Vera put her hand on his to arrest him.

"Well, Colonel," she purred, "what my dear friend Charlie is trying to say – and let me add I agree with him – is that your young Lieutenant is immensely talented. In fact, I would be most grateful if you would allow him to accompany me this evening. Just for one song," she added quickly as Charlie Kunz bristled beside her.

Smiling from ear to ear as he considered how such an event would reflect favourably on him and on *his* OCTU. He let the dialogue play out in his mind: *Of* course *we turn out first class officers here! But that's* not all *we do! Why, just the other day I personally gave one of our young men a leg up on a professional musical career—after this current business is concluded, naturally! 'How?' you ask. Oh, it was nothing much, really. I prevailed upon my close personal friends Vera Lynn and Charlie Kunz—yes, The King of the Pianists' Melodies, that's the one...*

The Colonel promptly stood, offering Miss Lynn his arm. Without a further word to Charlie Kunz he escorted her from the head table to the raised platform that served as a stage halfway down the hall where Lieutenant Lawes was seated at the grand piano, softly but quite contentedly playing some of his own favourite pieces.

He had seen them rise and leave the head table. He had assumed that the Colonel was going to introduce her to some of the dignitaries— politicians and senior officers seated at the next table. When they walked right past it with merely a few nods and smiles his curiosity was mildly piqued. When they strode past the second table without even a glance at its occupants, he realized that they were both looking directly at and coming directly toward *him*!

Pulse quickening, he was relieved to note, when he allowed his attention to revert briefly to his playing, that he had been maintaining the proper tempo. Could this really be happening? Was he about to meet *the* Vera Lynn in person? What would Rene think of *that*? What would... *Don't get ahead of yourself upstart. She has probably recognized a distant cousin at a table at the back of the hall and....*

They had the good grace to allow him to finish the piece he was playing – a Chopin waltz – before they approached within speaking distance. Harold pushed back the piano bench, turned to face his exalted visitors and stood smartly to attention.

"Lieutenant Lawes," the Colonel began, conversationally.

"Sir!" Harold responded automatically before the Colonel could complete what he had been about to say.

"Yes, well... a-hemmh..." the Commandant sputtered, at one and the same time annoyed at the interruption to the carefully mentally rehearsed speech that he had composed en route from the head table and pleased by *his* trainee's *(Graduate! Graduate! This is after all a* passing out *ceremony!)* show of correct military discipline and respect.

Recovering his poise, he continued. "I have the honour to present," he pontificated, turning to the glittering celebrity on his arm with a slight bow, "Miss Vera Lynn." As Vera took her hand from his arm and stepped toward Harold the Colonel glanced furtively toward the head table to be sure that everyone remaining there was watching. "Miss Lynn," he purred, stretching out his right arm in Harold's direction as if he were ushering the lady to her seat in a cinema, "our very own Lieutenant Lawes."

The gracious luminary smiled warmly and extended her hand. Harold didn't know whether to shake it, kiss it, or bow. Much to the delight of the assembled spectators Harold took the middle ground and was resoundingly cheered and applauded during and well beyond the too brief event. The Colonel, meanwhile, almost spinning about on his heels to acknowledge what he mistakenly assumed to be *his* accolades, was temporarily distracted while Harold quietly, for Vera Lynn's ears only, managed to spurt out something about how honoured he was to meet her. "... and my sister, Rene, will be absolutely thrilled..." he was saying, but before he could get another word out the Colonel's voice, raised to a pitch that ensured no one in the room could even pretend to ignore it, broke in.

"Ladies and gentlemen!" he intoned, in his best imitation of what he imagined might be the ringing pronouncements of a 19th century town crier or at the very least the ring master at a circus. "It is my singular pleasure and honour..." (He paused for effect and was almost overcome by the unanticipated revelation that *this* must be what his literary friends called a *pregnant* pause.) The unnatural silence in the huge room slowly penetrated his consciousness and he brought himself up short. "Ladies and gentlemen!" he repeated himself, *"Miss – Veeerah – Lynn!"*

Boot stomping and prolonged thunderous applause erupted, interspersed with shrill whistles and cat calls, effectively drowning out the rest of the Colonel's introduction. When the tumult showed no sign of letting up, he raised both arms, striking a pose he had seen some long-forgotten speaker adopt while standing on a soap box in Hyde Park. He was inordinately pleased with himself when the room abruptly quieted.

"Miss Lynn has graciously consented to sing..." Cheering erupted again, and it was clear that this time no amount of gesticulating on the part of the Commandant would avail to end it. The heart throb of British troops everywhere leaned close to speak to Harold, practically shouting to make herself heard. "What would you like to play for me?"

"My signature tune, "Whispering," in E flat," he replied without hesitation. "Would that be acceptable?"

The urbane songstress simply smiled, nodded, and gestured for him to take his place at the piano. As he did so, she glided to the front of the little stage, bringing the palms of her hands together in front of her as if about to pray. The sudden profound silence in the grand ballroom of the Chine hotel was truly awesome.

The applause began turning into groans and shouts of "Encore!" and "More!" when Harold, having kissed Vera Lynn's hand a second time, turned, stepped down from the stage, and sauntered away toward one of the exits. They wanted another song. They wanted a hundred more songs from their living goddess of song. Harold didn't even notice the mood change reflected in the raised voices. He was walking on air. He had played for *the* Vera Lynn and she, with her magnificent voice, had made his signature tune sound like... well, like nothing that his sister Irene, (bless her,) had ever come close to!

Suddenly, he could hear the solid thudding of his own boots on the polished wooden floor. Startled, he stopped and turned about, realizing even as he did so that the magnificent Vera Lynn had again quieted the throng with a simple gesture.

"And now, ladies and gentlemen!" her powerful voice carried to every corner of the vast room. She looked to the head table where, virtually forgotten, Charlie Kunz sat, arms crossed, and lower lip thrust out like that of a pouting child. Vera spread her arms out toward him in invitation, smiled broadly as only she could smile and shouted: "Clap hands! Here comes Charlie!"

Harold enthusiastically joined in the rhythmic clapping, which went on for at least a full minute before Charlie finally rose from his chair, adjusted the expression on his face to a professional smile, and deigned to accept the lady's invitation. And to acknowledge his adoring audience.

Ninety minutes later under the approving smiles of both Vera Lynn and the Commandant, Charlie Kunz, The Piano Medley King, and Harold Lawes, newly commissioned Second Lieutenant in the RASC, were seen shaking hands.

IN THE DRAWING ROOM
December 30, 1940

"They say that the glow of the fires reflecting on the clouds could be seen from as far away as Northampton," Cecil marvelled.

"'A conflagration that, in the humble opinion of this correspondent, must surely rival that of 1666.'" The newspaper snapped in Walter's pudgy fingers. "Now, when he refers to himself as 'this correspondent'," he mused, "is that first person or third person, hmn?" he mused

Cecil made a 'tisking' sound with the side of his mouth. "Nasty things, incendiaries. The firefighters I talked to this morning claim that the fires spread so fast they've no hope of containing them to a small area. And it's the devil's own work, they said, trying to put out the flames."

"Especially, I should think, when the water supply fails," said Walter, "which is what happened last night, it says here." He read on in silence for a few moments. "Well, damn it all to hell!" he suddenly sputtered.

"Say what?" asked Cecil.

"Seems our own engineers felt obliged to do some of Jerry's work for him," Walter scowled. "They blew up a number of buildings on purpose, trying to create fire breaks!"

"Nothing for it, I suppose," Cecil moped. "Did it do any good?"

"St. Paul's survived again," Walter told him, lowering his paper.

The two old friends exchanged half-hearted smiles.

O.C.T.U. Graduating Class
February 1941

Lieutenant Lawes

5

SOMEWHERE IN SCOTLAND
March 1941 through October 1942

At this point, Harold's military career took an unexpected turn. The mysterious Major from Special Operations with the eloquent support of the assessment reports written by Harold's instructors at OCTU had reached a decision that fateful day, a few weeks back, when he had watched Harold's performance on the firing range. In the course of the afternoon of interviews that the Major had conducted with Harold's instructors he had learned that, throughout his training at OCTU and before, Lieutenant Lawes had excelled at virtually every task required of him, but especially in the areas of small arms and unarmed combat.

The morning following that oh-so-memorable evening when he had played the piano for Vera Lynn, Lieutenant Lawes was summoned to the Commandant's office. He was ushered in the moment he arrived and stood to attention as the door was closed behind him. Seated across from the Colonel was a Major whose insignia Harold did not recognize—and he was sure he had memorized them all.

"Ahemm," the Colonel cleared his throat. "Yes, well now, Lieutenant Lawes. Major Simmons here has a proposition for you. It's all strictly voluntary, you understand. The Service Corps will be loathe to lose one of their..."

He broke off as the Major rose from his chair and crossed the room towards Harold in two enormous strides. Startled, Harold almost took a step back but recovered as the Major extended his hand and flashed a smile. "Strictly voluntary," the Major confirmed. "Let me tell you something about Combined Operations. We're officially known as the Special Service Brigade, and we're recruiting individuals from units all over the country..."

Thus, for the better part of the next two years Harold found himself in Scotland as a member of and a Senior Instructor to a rather special group of soldiers—the British Commandos.

After the London area and the south coast, Scotland was a relative oasis of calm. When the *Luftwaffe* sent planes this far north from their bases in Norway it was usually after industrial targets and not a remote training camp that their intelligence had probably not yet identified. Harold enjoyed his new assignment tremendously. While as a non-commissioned officer (NCO) he had been given responsibilities that entailed some training of others, mostly he had been on the receiving end of the training. He was still less than happy about not being in the thick of things at the front, but at least now he felt he was making a meaningful contribution. It certainly beat washing lorries or memorizing military acronyms! And he liked the fact that here there was an unusual degree of informality, especially among his cadre of fellow Instructors.

Red tape and paperwork were relegated to the past—or at least to someone else. And rank didn't count for as much as what one knew or could do. Although only a lowly Second Lieutenant, Harold was by no means the most junior in rank among the Instructors' unit, which included several Captains and Majors but an equal contingent of NCOs. So while a Lieutenant Colonel was nominally in charge of the entire operation, (or at least the part of it to which he was posted,) it was generally acknowledged that for all practical purposes, the head of the Instructors' unit was Staff Sergeant J.J. Critchley.

'Jay-Jay' was a short, barrel-chested Liverpudlian with bulging biceps and thigh muscles, a broad accent, and an indefatigable if sometimes wicked sense of humour. Standing only five-feet six-inches tall, he was undeniably the strongest, fittest, and most agile man Harold had ever encountered.

"Awfficers don' fawll any 'arder than oother ranks, *Suh*!" Jay-Jay was fond of reminding Harold every time he threw him to the mat during their sparring practices in unarmed combat. On the firing range he was almost Harold's equal with a handgun. When it came to the sniper's rifle or any of the automatic weapons, he was the better of the two by a slim margin.

In full gear Jay-Jay could run up and down the Scottish mountainsides all day long and never look worse for wear than had he been out for a casual stroll in the park before dinner. "Don' be late fuor tea, lads!" he would encourage those still climbing up as he was heading back down to camp. He could lift and hold the back axle of a fifteen-hundred weight lorry three inches off the ground and hold it there for ten minutes with nothing but his bare hands and his strong back while cheerfully admonishing: "Change bloody tyre right quick, now, else I may 'tyre' of this and let drop on yewer toes!"

Nothing fazed him. After only one practice drop from the parachute tower, he couldn't wait to do the real thing from a troop plane. When they practised amphibious landings at night he would be first out of the landing craft and single-handedly manhandle the awkward boat onto the beach while others were still slipping over the sides into the water. Once, his initial tug was so violent it sent one of his mates sprawling unceremoniously into frigid waist-deep water. "What's the almighty bloody rush, Jay-Jay?" demanded the unfortunate Commando. "Terra firma, me lad, terra firma!" Jay-Jay responded. "P'raps *you* knows 'ow to swim, but I likes me feet on terra firma!" In the common mess the instructors shared so they could discuss and compare notes on the progress of their charges, his favourite after-dinner trick was to unbend the horseshoe of a Clydesdale until it was a perfectly straight, flat, bar of iron, then bend it back into shape again explaining: "Jus' think o' it as wun of 'err 'itler's little eighty-eights, wot's bin givin' you a bit 'o trubble an' bother."

When Harold and Jay-Jay finally saw their first in-the-field action together near dawn on the bitterly cold morning of March 4th, 1941, it proved in some ways, to be disappointingly anticlimactic. Five hundred strong, accompanied by fifty-odd 'sappers" from the Royal Engineers and an equal number of volunteers from the German-occupied country they were about to raid, the tension among these elite troops was palpable. They climbed down rope netting into landing craft that had been lowered from the two cross-channel ferries that had been pressed into service for the occasion and slowly made their way toward shore. Their objectives, seemingly innocuous, were fish processing factories on the Lofoten Islands lying off the northwest coast of Norway.

"You mean to say we're goin' to all this trouble just to take his pickled herring off Jerry's menu?" one NCO had quipped to general amusement at one of the first pre-mission briefings.

"Indeed, you might say that," acknowledged the man from MI6 standing in front of the huge projected map at the back wall of the room, rhythmically slapping his thigh with the long pointer he held. "Or you might say we're going to deprive Jerry of something even more valuable. Herring oil!" The scattered nervous chuckling quickly quieted when they saw the stern look on his face. Christ! He wasn't joking!

"Herring oil and codfish oil," the Foreign Intelligence Officer continued, raising his voice. "Jerry needs it to make glycerine, which in turn is used to make explosives!"

Less than restrained murmuring erupted everywhere in the big room. The lecturer held up both hands for quiet and the hubbub swiftly subsided. "And if it makes you feel any better, yes, we will also be taking an important supply of foodstuffs off of their 'menu', as you called it." He leaned forward bracing both arms on the table in front of him. "You may not realize just *how* important."

He paused with deliberate drama, looking from face to expectant face, briefly capturing the suddenly intense gazes of as many of the men as possible.

"The flesh of these fishes is, of course, important. But it might surprise you to learn that these same fish oils are also the primary source of something Jerry depends upon to keep his troops healthy. From the oils they extract the vitamins A and D. These essential vitamins, in the form of pills, are regularly issued to German troops on the front line to supplement what we have every reason to believe is a diet having no more nutritional value than that of our own troops... enjoy."

In the cold pre-dawn with the Lofoten Islands looming ever closer, more than a few of the Commandos, huddling below the gunwales of the ponderously chugging landing craft, expecting at any moment to fired upon, were thinking back to that big, warm briefing room and the laughter they had shared thanks to the dry humour of the man from MI6.

Imagine their surprise when, rather than being subjected to the hostile fire they had anticipated, they were instead greeted by small groups of cheering islanders who came out of their houses to help the landing parties ashore. Encountering minimal resistance, they took over two hundred German merchant seamen prisoner, demolished the fish processing factories, and were back on board the waiting ferries shortly after the noon hour. As a bonus, more than 300 of the locals returned with them as recruits for the Free Norwegian forces based in Britain.

"Bit of a romp, neh?" said Jay-Jay, punching Harold on the shoulder as they descended the ferry's gangplank, safely back on friendly soil. "Pity there wasnuh a piano fer ye to twiddle with."

Harold's response was to push Jay-Jay's helmet down over his eyes and shoulder his friend off the gangplank. Fortunately, they were near the bottom of the span with less than a foot of drop to the cement. *Might just as well have been two or three feet*," Harold thought to himself with a mental shrug as Jay-Jay – possibly having anticipated Harold's reaction – deftly turned the shove into a simple side-step and kept on marching. He didn't even bother to tilt his helmet back: but Harold could tell that his friend was grinning from ear to ear.

They were markedly less jovial about the whole affair two days later when it was reported that representatives of the press had been on board the Lofoten ferries—by official invitation. Some of those gentlemen of the press were claiming that the raid had been nothing but a photo op, a publicity stunt, pre-arranged by Churchill and Mountbatten to further their mutual desire to ensure that the Special Forces units were not disbanded.

Harold had just returned from a ten-day leave during which he had helped Charlie and Violet move into a smaller house on Lennard Road in New Beckenham when in August, with a few of their comrades, he and Jay-Jay were part of a small support group of Commandos for a raid by Canadian and Free Norwegian troops on another Norwegian island. Spitsbergen was even farther north than the Lofotens and "just as blinkin' cold, thank-you-very-much," despite the time of year. Thankfully, this turned out to be yet another successful venture. A couple of earlier less than salutary Commando raids had brought on a new level of skepticism among many in the senior ranks – even the Chiefs of Staff – as to the efficacy of a Special Forces unit. This raid on Spitsbergen, resulting in the destruction of irreplaceable stores of coal and the capture of a German wireless crew, went a long way to re-enforcing Churchill's stubborn support of the concept.

On December 27th at yet another place in Norway, which Harold and Jay-Jay readily admitted to one another neither of them knew how to pronounce – Vâsøy, or Vaagso – they teamed up again. After wading ashore in the early hours, shivering constantly despite their exertions of more than four hours, slipping and slithering through the bleak, snow-covered terrain from one indistinguishable building to another, their attack group came away with more than 100 prisoners. Jay-Jay came away with a burst eardrum. The muzzle of the German officer's Luger was within half an inch of his ear when it discharged as Jay-Jay was plunging his knife into the enemy's throat.

Twenty of their comrades had been killed and nearly three times that number had been wounded. Nevertheless, this raid, too, was judged by the powers-that-be to have been a success. And in truth, despite the grievous losses, while neither man said so out loud, each felt good about what had been achieved. The British Commandos had irrefutably established their worth. Without hubris both Harold and Jay-Jay felt that the two of them had made some small contribution to that accomplishment.

Harold next saw action in France on March 27th, 1942. Jay-Jay had been relegated to home-based duty, resuming his Instructor's role back in Scotland. The strategic target of the Commandos on this occasion was the dry dock at St. Nazaire near the mouth of the Loire River in Brittany. It was the only one in enemy hands in the entire north Atlantic big enough to take the *Tirpitz*, a German battleship currently somewhere in Norway and imbued, one might say, with a well-earned reputation.

For days in the aftermath of that Commando raid on St. Nazaire the Allied journalists and newscasters heaped praise upon Lord Louis Mountbatten and what had become *his* Combined Operations. Only 214 of the 611 Commandos and sailors who had set out on the mission on March 26th returned to British shores, but the primary objective had been achieved. With its heroic Captain at the helm, *HMS Campbeltown*, an aging destroyer packed with explosives on time-delay fuses, had run the gamut of the decimating barrage of German shore batteries and lodged itself in the outer gates of the dry dock. The *Campbeltown* blew up on March 28th killing almost 400 of the enemy and putting the dry dock out of commission for the remainder of the war.

Harold had been one of the lucky ones. The motorized launch in which he was crouching with his platoon of Commandos as they made their precarious way up the estuary of the Loire was among the first to be hit by the shore batteries. A dozen of his men had been wounded and one killed outright. The tiny bit of shrapnel that had pierced Harold's right temple and rendered him unconscious had done so before his landing craft got anywhere near to shore. Along with most of his platoon he was safely evacuated without having fired a shot.

Being young, healthy, and exceptionally fit meant that Harold's convalescence took no more than a few days. The shrapnel had not penetrated very deeply. The doctor had needed to make only a tiny incision to remove it with a fine pair of tweezers. He proudly boasted to his patient that within a month there would likely not even be a visible scar. But now Harold suffered from recurrent migraines and had to wear prescription glasses. And like Jay-Jay, he was restricted to home-based duties. Over the months that ensued, having resumed their familiar roles as Instructors of new recruits for the Commandos, Harold and Jay-Jay cemented their relationship as fast friends. Even so, Harold was not immune to Jay-Jay's irrepressible, caustic humour.

At a graduation party for one group of newly anointed Commandos Harold was playing "There, I've Said It Again," on the piano, embellishing it unnecessarily with runs and glissandos as the gathered soldiers sang lustily along. Just as he finished the piece and sat back Jay-Jay rushed up to him and slammed down the keyboard cover with enough force to set every string vibrating as though the entire instrument had been dropped from a great height. The room fell silent as the massive reverberating chord slowly diminished in volume.

"If I've told you once, I've told you an 'undred times, *Suh!* You keep them wiggly digits attached to yooer 'ands, *Suh*! You will shooerly be wantin' 'em if you ever actually get to see action again, *Suh!*"

Because of Jay-Jay and because there was a sense of genuine accomplishment with each class of graduates, Harold still enjoyed his time with the Commandos in Scotland's rugged and oft' times inhospitable hills and glens. Yet even here there were casualties of the war.

In one case a fellow instructor in unarmed combat was attempting to demonstrate how to disarm an opponent who was charging at him with fixed bayonet. The instructor misjudged his timing. The bayonet entered the inside of his forearm an inch above the wrist, tearing its way up to and through the elbow. (*"No bloody good!"* Harold murmured to himself, unconsciously employing one of his father's favourite expressions.)

In another case, during a practice session on the firing range the breech of an anti-tank rifle exploded, blinding the man firing it and taking two fingers off the hand of the man next to him. (*"No bloody good!"*)

Potentially the most disastrous event, when one trainee fumbled with and dropped a live grenade into the sandbagged cubicle from which he was supposed to lob it, resulted in nothing more than a sprained wrist. Both the trainee and his instructor had the presence of mind to dive over the sandbags in front of them before the grenade exploded. Unfortunately for the instructor he landed badly and thus the sprained wrist. (*"No bloody good!"*)

During this period, Harold got home on leave only infrequently, (before all home leaves for his group were cancelled in June of 1942) and never for very long. His parents and sisters, when he managed to see them, were a constant source of love and warmth, effusive in their praise of his progress and his rise to officer status. Betty, however, was disturbingly less amorous than he might have hoped. (*"No bloody good, at-oll!"*)

On October 18th 1942 – the very day that Hitler issued his infamous order that all British Commandos taken prisoner were to be summarily executed – the man who had successfully recruited Harold and many others like him for the Commandos paid a visit to Harold's unit. Major Simmons was now a full Colonel but had lost none of his charm.

"By all accounts you've done rather well by us, Lieutenant Lawes." Colonel Simmons placed special emphasis on 'Lieutenant' as he reached across the desk smiling and deposited two shiny brass pips in front of Harold. "You have earned these, I dare say. You can put them up with their brothers at once, if you like." His smile grew even broader. "Your promotion to full Lieutenant is retroactive to the first of June." He rose and came around from behind the desk extending his hand, the smile never wavering. "Let me be the first to congratulate you!" They shook hands. "Now, I should like to talk to you," Colonel Simmons continued, turning away to resume his seat.

"Déjà vu," thought Harold. *"This man is going to change my life... again!"*

Notice of his reassignment to the RASC brought mixed emotions. Underlying it all was a sense of hurt. Were they trying to tell him that he was no longer good enough for the Commandos? ("Good gracious, no, Old Boy! It's not like that at all!*)* Then why did you have to mention the migraine headaches? (You must understand that the demands of this conflict are in a continuous state of flux, and that your many talents... we are not discounting the enormous contribution you have already made and could, undoubtedly, continue to make in your present capacity...")

Colonel Simmons was damn smooth, damn good at his job, you had to give him that. ("...at the present time, combined with the skills you have perfected with us, your other talents are potentially even more valuable elsewhere.")

I've learned how to kill a man with my bare hands! Harold thought. *I was a banker and an accountant before all this. What bloody use are those skills against the enemy?*

On the one hand it meant saying good-bye to Jay-Jay and the other members of the Commandos Instructors' cadre. They had developed into a very close-knit team, and he had grown to feel that he formed an integral part of that team. What's more, when as a group the Instructors' corps listened in on the wireless to the most recent exploits of some of their graduates, it filled them all with a sense of pride and accomplishment.

On the other hand, this might be his last chance to once again be in on the real thing!

A surprisingly subdued Jay-Jay did the honours at Harold's going away party. The Colonel and one or two other administrative types were there but the makeup of the ensemble was primarily his fellow Instructors. Only when they roasted him did Jay-Jay live up to expectations.

"'Ere's an *awfficer*," Jay-Jay began. "Wot don' know 'is elbow frum 'is ass 'ole! An' the powers wot be 'ave decided, in their inf'nit' wisdum, to send 'im into the thick o' things! An' if that's not bad enough... 'e'll actuooly 'ave an 'hole *platooon* of innocent young men to look awfter!"

The mock diatribe extended for more than five minutes but by the end of it, Jay-Jay's eyes were brimming with tears of affection. Finally, he invited Harold to join him at the podium.

"God alone knows why but the lads 'ere 'ave determined that they'd like you to 'ave sumthin' by which to remember us. We shure as 'ell won' forget *you*, you twiddley-fingered coot. If I may remind you, *Suh*... keep them digits...! If I've told you an 'undred times...!" Jay-Jay had to pause to blow his nose. "Anyway, this 'ere's from all the lads, an' may it serve you well."

It was one of the Colt .45 automatic pistols, with three spare clips and two hundred rounds of ammunition.

IN THE DRAWING ROOM
August 20, 1942

"Criminal, Walter, that's what it is! Absolutely criminal." For once, it was Cecil who had his dander up. He was pacing back and forth in front of the long wooden settee which stood below the windows looking out onto Pall Mall.

"It's one thing for the Ruskies to throw men into the line like so much cannon fodder... there's hundreds o' millions of them and their Generals obviously don't put much stock in the value of a human life. But for *our* Generals to treat *our* soldiers like that..." Cecil plonked himself down hard on the settee. "Criminal, I say!" He was referring to the disastrous Anglo-Canadian raid on Dieppe that had cost 1,027 dead and 2,034 taken as prisoners of war.

Walter wisely held his peace waiting for his friend to regain his composure. When he judged that Cecil's breathing had returned to normal – that the slender man was still distracted was clearly evident – Walter levered himself out of his wing chair, crossed the room, and sat down beside him on the settee.

"Cecil," he said quietly. "Cecil," he repeated when there was no response. *"Cecil!"* he finally bellowed at the same time slapping his friend's thigh with the back of his hand, determined to bring the man out of his reverie.

Cecil almost jumped out of his skin. "What's got into you then?" he demanded sharply.

"Cecil," said Walter, his voice calm and quiet once more. "This is not like you. Not like you at all."

Cecil's slim, white eyebrows knitted into a scowl. "Whatever are you going on about?" He stood up and took a few aimless steps into the room.

"What am *I* going on about?" an exasperated Walter asked. "Have you been listening to yourself for the last five minutes? Hmn?"

Cecil spun about to face him, his head thrust forward like a bird with a short skinny neck. "Do you mean to tell me that you *approve* of what those incompetent...?"

Walter held up both hands, pleading for his friend to remain calm. "I agree completely and unequivocally with your assessment."

"I should bloody well hope so!" came the rejoinder.

"But Cecil, that's not the point," said the big man as placidly as he could, trying not to show his annoyance. "The point is, old man, you are not behaving normally."

Cecil bit his tongue to stop a stinging retort and cocked his head to one side, fixing Walter with his best imitation of a Doberman trying to decide where to bite his victim first. Walter took this as a sign that he was to continue.

"Look, you remember last May when I was all in a tizzy over the loss of the *Hood*? Only three survivors out of a crew of more than 1,400?"

"Of course, I remember!" spat Cecil. "You ranted and raved at the top of your lungs for three days... until our lads got even by sinking the *Bismark*. What are you getting at?"

"Do you remember how *you* behaved at the time? Hmn?" Walter persisted.

"Same as I always do, I suppose," Cecil reflected. Having been drawn into a conversation with his old friend his anger was, if not dissipating, at least being held in check.

"Precisely!" Walter loudly smacked his own knee in triumph. "Even then you found dozens of reasons, however irrelevant or insignificant, to shine a positive light on the overall situation. And every time I paused for breath you would fling one at me, like a zookeeper locked in a cage with a hungry tiger flinging bits of meat to keep the beast at bay."

"Did I really act like... what you just said?" queried Cecil, his face the picture of innocence itself.

"Damn straight, old boy!" said Walter. "And that's what I'm getting at. For you that was normal behaviour, hmn? This... this unbridled, endless tirade..." He gestured for permission to be allowed to finish because Cecil was about to pounce. "Look, all I'm saying is this is not like you, Cecil... and I don't like it, not one bit."

Expressionless, Cecil stared at the ceiling for few moments. Slowly, his lips pressed firmly together, the corners of his mouth turned up. For a moment he looked for all the world like the silent film star Stan Laurel.

"Well then," he said. "What am I to do about it? *Hmn?*" he added in mock imitation of his dear friend.

"Tell you what," said Walter, a sly smile creeping onto his face. "Let *me* play at being *you*. I'll tell you all the really good things I can think of and you... well, you just listen... *you know*," he appended, unable to resist returning the jibe.

Cecil walked back to their customary table and sat down, motioning for Walter to join him. "Pray begin."

"Churchill!" Walter slapped the tiny table with the flat of his palm, punctuating his one-word exclamation.

Cecil's forehead wrinkled. "What about him?"

"Vote of confidence—overwhelming vote of confidence in the House of Commons last month. And we're both agreed..."

Cecil rolled his eyes. Walter had only recently (and grudgingly at that) admitted that the Prime Minister was not 'just another bloody politician.' "And we are *both* agreed," Walter continued with deliberate emphasis, "that he is Britain's 'Man of the Hour', a true War Leader. Hmn?" He looked hopefully at his friend. If he couldn't elicit a positive response with his first (and, he had felt sure, his most puissant argument) then his role playing wasn't going to go very far.

"Conceded." Cecil gave a brief nod, crossed his arms, and sat back in his chair.

"Alexander!" said Walter immediately, again slapping the little table. "Oh, and, uh, um..." his hand remained poised above the table, so Cecil said nothing. "Montgomery!" The hand came down with a satisfying thwack and Walter's expression, Cecil mused, was downright cherubic.

"Oh, well done!" Cecil declared theatrically. "I feared for a moment that I... that is to say, *I*, as you are representing me... was incapable of uttering more than a single word in any argument I may have postulated in the past."

He was enjoying this. Keeping a straight face, he invited: "Do elaborate, Sir, that I might be the beneficiary of your unparalleled wisdom."

Walter had the bit between his teeth now and was not easily to be put off. "Real soldiers, both of them. Commanders tried in combat and true. Auchinleck was no slouch I'll allow... but Ritchie?"

"And so...?" Cecil teased. Ex-infantry himself, he understood exactly where Walter was headed.

"So…" Walter, warming to his subject, was in the process of discovering much to his own surprise that he rather liked playing at being Cecil. No that wasn't it exactly. The rush of adrenaline he felt at that moment emanated from something far more visceral.

"So, I respectfully submit we will soon have that Desert Fox Rommel running for his hide-y-hole!" he finished.

Cecil finally allowed himself to smile. "For a bluejacket I must confess, Walter, you display an uncommon appreciation of the footslogger's enduring occupational predicament. The lack of competent leadership." He lightly tapped the table with his fingertips. Point to Walter.

The retired Royal Navy Commander was tempted briefly to sit back and bask in his friend's glowing compliment – coming from Cecil it *was* noteworthy – but experience demanded that this was the moment to close in for the kill.

"The Americans!" he confidently thundered. "And with that, your Lordship…" mimicking a solicitor before the King's bench, "… I rest my case."

"Yes, well…" began Cecil's taciturn reply.

"Bloody hell, man!" Walter could not constrain himself. "They're *in* it at last! And the Yanks are bringing with them *more* ships, *more* tanks, *more* artillery – not to mention *troops* – than we could ever have hoped for in our *wildest* dreams!"

"I cannot dispute you there, Walter." Cecil signalled to Stilson. Time for their afternoon glasses of port. "Still, I should be gratified to hear that their troops were physically involved in the actual conflict rather than making a nuisance of themselves chatting up and seducing our young ladies with cigarettes and silk stockings here at home."

Unbeknownst to Cecil and Walter on the afternoon immediately preceding their heated dialogue, the Yanks had in fact committed a sizable number of their troops to battle. It was dubbed Operation Torch, the Allied invasion of North Africa under the American General Dwight D. Eisenhower. It was, at the time, the largest amphibious invasion force that had ever been launched in the history of warfare.

6

NORTH AFRICA
November 1942 through April 1943

With Harold as its Lieutenant, F Platoon of 105 Corps Bridge Company left from Gourock, Scotland on November 27, 1942 on the Polish ship *M.S. Sobieski,* and after a wandering, befuddling but otherwise uneventful 11 days at sea, it arrived at Phillippeville, Algeria at 0930 hours. As they disembarked at 1300 hours, they were issued their first British Military Authority (BMA) money. They formed up smartly and accompanying themselves with a rousing rendition of "Bless 'em All!" quick-marched all the way to No. 3 Transit Camp, arriving at 1600 hours—in plenty of time to pitch their tents and locate the mess hall before darkness fell.

Although it was relatively quiet in the transit camp, few of them got much sleep that night. The desert fleas saw to that. In the morning the flies arrived accompanied by two low-flying Messerschmitts whose strafing runs happily proved largely ineffectual. After a breakfast of beans and sausages, the platoon assembled in a sort of natural amphitheatre behind the mess tent for a briefing on the local conditions. The briefing was in essence an enumeration of warnings boiled down to a list of 'dos and don'ts.' These included such precautionary measures as using animals to test the wells for poison and giving your boots a vigorous shake in the morning to dislodge any overnight visitors—like scorpions!

All the news was good news. The Allies had finally relieved the beleaguered garrison at Tobruk and had pressed on to take Benghazi. It was the fifth and last time in the course of the desert war that that city would change hands. The New Zealand Division and the 7th Armoured Division had Rommel's back against the wall at El Agheila. It was widely put about that the vaunted Afrika Korps was on its last legs because the Allies now commanded superiority both in the air and on the Mediterranean, which meant that few if any supplies were getting through to the enemy from Europe.

For the next few days the soldiers of newly arrived F Platoon settled into a make-work routine, cleaning and oiling their weapons repeatedly, filling in latrine trenches and digging new ones, attending boring lectures on personal hygiene, assembling Bailey bridges over imaginary waterways, and then dismantling them. Finally, exactly one week after they had first set foot in North Africa, their vehicles arrived. Feeling curiously relieved, Lieutenant Lawes contentedly made the appropriate entry in his War Diary: "*Strength, 29 vehicles, 8 motorcycles, 1 officer, 57 other ranks.*"

As they pulled out of Phillippville en route to Bône, Annaba, where they would set up camp on their own for the first time, a sign at the side of the road on the outskirts of town reminded them: "Dust draws mortar fire! Drive slow!" Other signs posted on each side of the road virtually every 50 yards simply read: "UXBs" or sometimes "Mines."

Within a few short weeks more than a quarter of the vehicles were out of service and more than a third of the men were suffering from dysentery or scabies or severe sunburn or some other debilitating disease. (*No bloody good!*) Harold seemed to spend half his time visiting his men in field hospitals. It wasn't until mid-February, now based in El Kef, Tunisia, that they were back up to full strength, and he was never quite sure how they had managed to survive in the interim.

By early March they were in Ksour and with the Afrika Korps on the run it began to look as though the month would turn out to be relatively (and mercifully) uneventful. In fact, by the end of the month Harold was just beginning to feel that he had the situation under control when he lost five men and two lorries to a strafing run by a lone Stuka dive bomber. These were the first he had lost to enemy fire and he was devastated. (*No bloody good!*) That same day a close friend, Captain Whittly, was killed. He had been walking in front of the lead vehicle of a bridging detachment, trying to spot and clear land mines when one of them blew up in his face. Also that day, he had received a disturbing letter from his mother hinting that his wife, Betty, was "not behaving as she should." (*No bloody good, at-oll!*)

Through April Harold saw more horrors than he could count or cared to remember. The urge to retch was an almost constant companion. Whether Allied troops or enemy, the unholy dread was unequivocal. Men enveloped in flame, running, screaming, from shattered tanks or armoured cars. Men with fingers or hands, arms or legs blown completely off. Men sitting in pools of their own blood and excrement desperately trying, vainly, to hold in their intestines. Human heads lying by the by the side of the road with no body anywhere in sight.

God? Whose side are you on?

He had lost 14 more men to the enemy: three dead, eleven wounded. Eight of the latter casualties had occurred in a single incident when a detachment of a dozen vehicles was caught in a barrage from a pair of the dreaded German ten-barreled mortars they called Moaning Minnies. Most of those wounded had been horribly scarred, not by shrapnel but by flying rock splinters. Nearly twice that number – 27 in all – were judged unfit for duty due to one disease or another. Indeed, few of the men could honestly be rated completely free from infection or FFI.

His back ached. His head throbbed remorselessly with migraines. And, like many others in this God-forsaken backwash, he was suffering severely from malaria. The unbridled self-confidence he had known back home was rapidly evaporating. He was beginning to feel hopeless and utterly miserable.

Lieutenant Lawes and his N.C.O.'s
F Platoon, November 1942

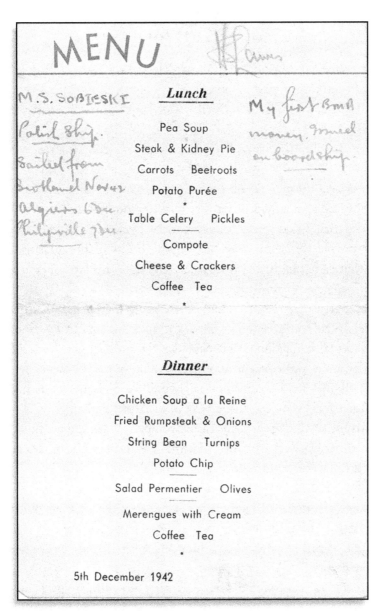

MENU

H. Lawns

M.S. SOBIESKI

Polish ship.

Sailed from
Scotland Nov 42
Algiers 6 Dec
Philipville 7 Dec.

Lunch

Pea Soup

Steak & Kidney Pie

Carrots   Beetroots

Potato Purée

*

Table Celery   Pickles

Compote

Cheese & Crackers

Coffee   Tea

*

My first BMA
money, issued
on board ship.

Dinner

Chicken Soup a la Reine

Fried Rumpsteak & Onions

String Bean   Turnips

Potato Chip

Salad Permentier   Olives

Merengues with Cream

Coffee   Tea

*

5th December 1942

Menu from M.S. Sobieski

IN THE DRAWING ROOM
June 16, 1942

It was a perfectly normal day outside, which is to say it was raining steadily, as it had been for the past 72 hours.

"I'll give you a word for it, Cecil." Walter stared into his empty teacup. "Atrocity!"

The slim old man across from him simply nodded his already bowed head.

"Another phrase that comes to mind: 'Man's inhumanity to man!'" Walter quoted somberly, still staring unseeing into his cup.

"Barbaric... iniquitous... unconscionable!" whispered Cecil, focusing on the purple veins standing out on the backs of his gnarled, bony hands that rested lightly, fingers intertwined, on his lap. "There are no words..."

Incredulous rumours that had been circulating for months had now been irrefutably confirmed. The Nazis had systematically embarked upon a brutal campaign of genocide to exterminate the Jews. Details of death camps and concentration camps that but a few weeks ago had been attributed to the conventional hyperbole of London's many 'rag' newspapers had even been the subject of debate in Parliament.

"Arrghh," Walter cleared his throat volubly. "What did we agree upon the last time you were in a funk? Hmn?" Cecil looked at his friend, the hint of a smile creasing the corners of his mouth.

"Always..." he blinked "... always let us find the bright side!"

Walter was quick to take up his cue. "We've got 'em on the run in North Africa!" he enthused.

"Aye..." Cecil responded regaining his spirits. "And the Ruskies are makin' a go of it!"

Late into the dreary, rain-soaked evening, unwilling to part company, with less than half a teaspoon of port evaporating in the bottom of their wine glasses, the two grizzled veterans of The War to End All Wars contested with one another to recall or to invent some reason to find the bright side. As the clock in the entrance hall struck one, Stilson, mustering all the discretion that his many years of service at the club had taught him, approached.

"Ah-hemn," he cleared his throat. And in the well- worn plea of publicans the width and breadth of England, though somewhat more reservedly, he suggested: "Time, gentlemen, please!"

PART 2

TOCCATA

7

HAMILTON, ONTARIO, CANADA
May 1943

"Come back tomorrow morning and I'll change the dressing for you. Meanwhile, go home and get some ice on it to keep the swelling down. You don't want any part of you growing bigger than it already is, now do you? I'll tell your foreman. Jenkins, isn't it?" she asked with a smile.

"Yes, that's right," said Bob Freeman, returning the smile. Freeman was in his late 50s. He stood four inches over six feet and weighed 260 pounds. "Thanks, Ruby. We're going to miss you around here. In fact, I don't know how we ever got along without you."

And he meant it. A veteran on the line at Dominion Glass Works, Freeman was the latest in a string of men and women who had come to realize that they could depend not only on Ruby's nursing skills but also on her constant good humour. Having a full-time nurse on the factory payroll was not common in 1943, and the enlightened management at Dominion Glass was accorded high marks by their workers for this innovation.

There had always been minor accidents—it was in the nature of the work, surrounded as they were by broken glass, hot molten glass, and heavy steel dies. But now, instead of going off to the hospital half-way across town or sending for the St. John's Ambulance people, in most cases the injured worker could simply walk into or be taken to the little infirmary on the second floor and be attended to immediately by a Registered Nurse. A pretty one at that.

And now she was going to be leaving them, for a while at least. Going 'over the pond' she was, where her nursing skills were more desperately needed than on the factory floor. Bob had seen her in her Lieutenant's uniform of the Canadian Red Cross Corps, and as he left the infirmary, he couldn't help being concerned for her, this tiny slip of a thing heading into a war zone. Tomorrow was to be her last day at the glass works.

Not unexpectedly, the gang at Dominion Glass gave her a bon voyage party. It was arranged towards the end of the first shift so that those coming on for the second shift could also attend. There were plenty of home-baked goodies served up with Coca-Cola in those squat, bumpy little bottles that they made right there in the factory. Everyone brought some sort of gift: nylons, cigarettes, chocolates, hand-knitted mittens, lily-of-the-valley soap, and talcum powder, which they knew was Ruby's favourite. The list went on and on. But the gift she treasured most was a poem written by one of the girls on the production line, Olga Mokolov. Olga read the poem aloud to a standing ovation.

Our Ruby

Throughout the years that I have worked,
She's been so good to me,
From cuts and pains she's never shirked,
And drank with us her tea.

I'm sure that others feel the same
Towards Ruby as I do.
She'll talk to us and play the game,
From Englishman to Jew.

Whenever we felt fairly low,
Upstairs to her we'd run,
And before you began to say hello,
We'd start to have some fun.

From the first day that she told us
That she was going away,
We never could believe it,
Until this very day.

And now that Ruby's going,
And we hope to see her again,
Her good looks she may be showing
To thousands of fighting men.

I hope that while she's far away,
By looking at this rhyme,
She'll carry on and thru' the day
She'll think of us sometime.

What many of the workers at Dominion Glass did not realize was that for the past few months Ruby had been going straight from work at the factory to the Hamilton General Hospital where she would grab a quick bite to eat before going on duty at 6:00 p.m. as an unpaid volunteer nursing sister.

It was a requirement of the Overseas Detachment of the Canadian Red Cross Corps that all applicants complete 200 hours of volunteer work before being eligible to go overseas. She had applied to both the Army and the Navy for a position as a nurse, and while each would have thankfully welcomed her services neither would commit to giving her a posting overseas. That's where she felt she was most needed and could do the most good in whatever capacity. So, when she learned that the Red Cross was sending welfare workers to England and even to North Africa, she joined immediately.

She was giving up a good job that paid very well indeed – almost $700.00 a year – for the opportunity to contribute meaningfully to the war effort. Admittedly, also for the prospect of adventure and the chance to travel. Still, as a volunteer she would receive an allowance of only $5.00 a week (plus room and board, which at the time sounded pretty good) from the Red Cross. Like all members of the Corps she was expected to cover all her other costs out of her own pocket, including the khaki uniforms she had ordered from Eaton's department store.

Ruby Georgina Cobbett, R.N., exactly five-feet one-inch tall in her stocking feet, weighing just under 100 pounds, was 29 years old and single. Her ash-blond hair, blue eyes, and slim figure combined to make quite an attractive package. She had turned down more proposals of marriage than she could number and was confident there would be others.

There was one still on the table to which she had recently been giving serious thought. The local pharmacist, Phillip Russel, had a wonderful sense of humour, and they seemed to share much in common. On the other hand, he was a full 18 inches taller than she was and every time she tried to visualize the two of them in bed together she broke out in uncontrollable fits of laughter.

She was in no hurry. She was enjoying her life and saw no reason to alter things for the time being. At least not until after she had had one truly great adventure in life. In a way she felt the war and the Red Cross Voluntary Aid Detachment (VAD), nursing division seemed to have come along for the express purpose of offering her that opportunity.

The eldest of nine children, she counted seven brothers and one sister. She lived at home with her parents and despite holding a full-time job she still found time to have fun. She loved to go dancing and play badminton and go on picnics or for long walks. The Hollywood movies that they showed at the Delta Cinema, just down the block from her parents' home on Hilda Avenue – a different one every week – enthralled her. She was a talented and enthusiastic bridge player. Friends, both male and female, were legion.

Her mother, Gladys, was loving and attentive, though with the youngest Cobbett, little Teddy, only two years old, much of her energy was understandably devoted to him at present. Harold, her father, while already in his 50s and with one glass eye, had joined the navy. As a Chief Petty Officer and Engine Room Artificer he was currently training sailors in the engine room of a submarine running back and forth between Halifax and Bermuda.

Harold and Gladys had both emigrated, independently, from England in 1905, she with her family at the age of 10. Harold, aged 14, had run away from home at his elder sister's house (their parents had died), lied about his age, and worked his way across the Atlantic on a tramp steamer. Both Harold and Gladys eventually ended up in Hamilton, Ontario.

It was while working as a chauffeur for the well-to-do Burgess family in Hamilton that Harold and Gladys met. One day Harold's generous employer had allowed him to use the car to drive round and visit his current girlfriend who, unbeknownst to him at the time, lived next door to Gladys. He parked the limousine on the street in front of his sweetheart's residence and went inside. A short while later he heard someone honking the car's horn and rushed outside greatly fearing that someone was tampering with his employer's valuable automobile.

He was relieved to see that it was only a pretty, young woman who was obviously admiring rather than tampering. Grand touring automobiles and their shiny silver horns with the big black rubber bulb on the end were still something of a novelty in Hamilton in 1913. So, when Gladys had seen the car from her front window she had hesitated only briefly before giving in to her curiosity and going outside to take a closer look. And to squeeze the big black rubber bulb.

As Harold approached, Gladys looked up from her inspection and smiled at him.

"Is this *yours?*" she asked innocently.

"Not yet," he answered with aplomb. "Would you like to go for a ride in it?"

Harold's erstwhile girlfriend quickly figured out why and where he had disappeared to that day as thereafter, he parked the car in front of Gladys' house.

Their courtship was spectacularly brief.

Harold also earned enough as a chauffeur to open his own auto garage and to put himself through school at the Hamilton Institute of Technology. He emerged with a Teaching Degree in Motor Mechanics.

Ruby's oldest brother, Harold Jr., with a degree in mechanical engineering, had moved to the United States a couple of years back and was employed in some hush-hush activity by the American federal government. Next in line, John or 'Jack' as he was more commonly called, had recently married and was off in Winnipeg, training as a gunner with the RCAF. The others – Pearl, (she was Peggy or Peg, to anyone who knew her well), Roy, Bill, Russel, and Don, were all still in school.

The following Monday after tearful farewells with her mother and her siblings – even two-year-old Teddy cried, though he probably didn't understand why – Ruby reported for duty. The training was brief but intensive. A mere four weeks later Ruby and her mates fastened their single pips onto their shoulder epaulets (though they remained officially civilians, these accorded them the courtesy of officer status), and boarded a train for Montreal, bound for a ship that would take them to England.

IN THE DRAWING ROOM
October 26, 1942

"Didn't I tell you? Hmn?" demanded Walter, smiling beatifically. He was quite full of himself. And the two snifters of brandy he had imbibed – he normally only had one and then only at Christmas – had gone a long way to enhancing his naturally ruddy complexion.

"Give it a rest, won't you?" complained Cecil, doing his utmost to keep a smile from his own face.

"I remember distinctly," Walter rumbled on undeterred. "In fact, I remember my exact words!" he beamed. "I said that we would soon have the Fox running for his hidey-hole! And look you now: *Al Ameneen*! Was I right or was I right? Hmn?"

"That's *El Alamein*, you know," Cecil corrected grimacing.

"Whatever," said Walter with a dismissive wave of his beefy hand. "We've run the blighters right into the Mediterranean! And now Sicily will provide a convenient stepping stone across that oversized pond. Hmn?"

"Convenient, did you say?" Cecil looked skeptical. "Well, I hope you're right, Walter. I hope you're right."

In the event, it took the Allies 38 days and cost 31,158 casualties to take Sicily. And, most of the defenders escaped to fight again.

Ruby at Dominion Glass Works

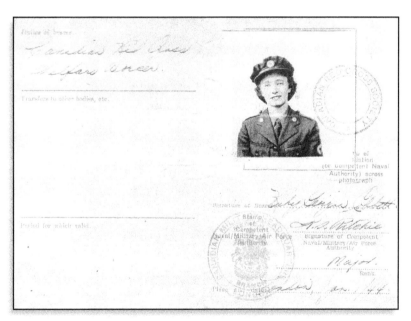

Certificate of Identity, October 1943

Ruby's first uniform

Sergean Gunner John Arthur Cobbett R.C.A.F.

8

MENZEL TEMIME, TUNISIA
May through July 1943

Advance units of the British 8th Army had just entered Tunis and the Americans, Bizerte. Resistance was collapsing far more quickly than many had dared to hope. Promoted acting Captain that morning and transferred to 235 Composite Company, Harold was not at all sure that he wanted the added responsibilities. He was running a high fever, undoubtedly a relapse of the malaria he had contracted in Algeria. He was physically exhausted and emotionally drained. He had a splitting migraine, an audit board to deal with at 0900 hours, and a company of almost 400 men and assorted vehicles to start moving by noon hour toward a place called Souk Ahras somewhere back in Algeria. From there, at 0500 the following morning, he was to take a detail to Ain el Asked to transport 800 prisoners of war, mostly Italians, to Mejaz el Bab.

Harold had been chosen over several other officers for this duty because he was fluent in French and spoke a little Italian. What's more, in the relatively short time he had been in North Africa he had already learned to speak and read enough Arabic that, together with his French, enabled him to communicate effectively with the locals.

The locals or the *wogs*, as most Allied troops had taken to calling them, at times seemed to be a population consisting almost entirely of thieves and horse traders. Every one of them carried at least two daggers – one openly the second concealed – with which they were disturbingly adept and which they were quick to use. Nothing was secure from them. Boots, blankets, cooking pots, laundry set out on a rock to dry—anything they *could* make off with, they did. They even stole tarpaulins right off the backs of the lorries and used them to make tents. They were neither for nor against the Allies. Their attitudes and behaviour had been the same toward the Italians and the Germans. They wouldn't stand up to you face to face. But you knew that you had to watch your back.

On Wednesday, May 12th, having been doggedly pursued by the British 6th Armoured Division, the remnants of the Axis troops in North Africa finally turned at bay in the hills around Enfidaville and fired off a last defiant salvo. They could run no farther. They had no more fuel. On May 13th, they formally surrendered. Scarcely two months later, Captain Harold Stanley Lawes was assigned as officer-in-charge of an Allied Victory March through Tunis. But to Harold at that time somehow it just didn't *feel* like victory—not at all.

Virtually one whole platoon was *hors de combat* under the disabling effects of their third dose of an anti-malaria drug called Atabrine. Corporal Burrows of Harold's old F Platoon had been killed by one of his own men in an accident on the firing range.

Their reluctant allies, the Americans, had managed to exacerbate the growing hard feelings, which had initially been engendered by their swaggering, their seemingly limitless supply of alcohol and cigarettes, their more generous and better tasting rations, their superior equipment, their apparent lack of military discipline. (*Bloody hell, they didn't even know when or how to salute!*) It didn't help either that every last one of these latecomers who had only been on hand for – what was it, six months? – boasted a chest full of ribbons. (Of course, everyone understood by now that the Americans awarded medals to their GIs for going to the loo!) Last week, the Americans had inadvertently bombed the Australians. Yesterday they had mistakenly shelled the Punjabis. And this morning their planes had sunk an Allied supply ship in the Mediterranean.

Even Mother Nature seemed to be conspiring to add to Harold's misery. Torrential rains would turn every road into almost impassable quagmires and every ditch and field into boot-sucking mud for days on end. At times it was so bad that even half-tracks and tanks floundered, their tracks churning great furrows in the reddish ooze. Too often mules or horses had to be conscripted to help pull a lorry out of glutinous muck up to its axles—or to transport the supplies that the lorries were supposed to deliver.

When the rains stopped the scorching sun would suck the moisture from the ground so violently that it was like being in a steam bath. And with the steam came the flies, later to be described in an official publication of the 8th Army as: "a filthy, pertinacious, excruciating pestilence." They got into his ears, eyes, nose, and mouth and swarmed onto his food so thickly that he could hardly see what was on the plate. The only relief from them was at night when the temperature plummeted so low that he would shiver, even wrapped in all three standard-issue blankets. The fleas obviously worked for the Hun, wriggling up and down his body at all hours of the day and night, biting at random. He even had lice! (Thank God for those typhus injections!) With only six pints of water per man per day, one daily sponge bath was all he permitted himself.

At dawn and again at dusk the mosquitoes came bringing tormenting itchy stings... and more malaria. The going would become easier for a day or two as the sun baked the mud into a hard cracked crust but then the *khamsin* or hot winds would start, seemingly devoid of oxygen and carrying clouds of choking dust. His migraine headaches were relentless.

Harold had to watch himself in front of the men. Forced smiles and a show of confidence he no longer really felt were becoming harder every day. Perhaps it would be easier, he told himself, if he could at least shoot back. All that training, all the hours and days of practice with weapons, from bayonet to anti-tank rifle, and he had yet to fire a shot at the enemy since his days with the Commandos. As Administrative Officer all he did was move troops and munitions, stores and equipment, build *bloody* bridges over nameless *bloody* 'wadis' and oversee the *bloody* logistics of *bloody* 235 Company's *bloody* personnel and materiel!

He couldn't remember the last time he'd had leave. He couldn't remember the last time he'd played or even *seen* a piano. It felt like a lifetime ago since he'd had a whiskey. He lit a cigarette. At least those were still available. Five per man per day.

IN THE DRAWING ROOM
June 3, 1943

"You know how difficult it is for this old sea dog to eat humble pie, Cecil, but I must confess, by God you had the right of it from the very beginning!" Walter wasn't really being all that penitent. He was simply acknowledging the emerging facts of the matter. "I never would have credited such a notion and even now if the evidence were not so preponderant... *Aeroplanes* in *sea* battles!"

"It's not entirely due to aeroplanes, you know," Cecil magnanimously allowed. "Although their Admiral Dönitz was certainly unstinting in his praise of their capabilities against his U-boats he also credited the increased number of escort ships, especially the speedy little corvettes. Oh, and he didn't know what it was called, but also that new depth charge weapon that you were explaining to me last week..."

"'The Hedgehog'" Walter offered helpfully.

"Quite," Cecil nodded. "In any event he has called off his wolf packs for the nonce," Cecil paused, drawing breath to continue. Walter, however, was the quicker on this occasion.

"And that is another very curious thing about this war," he mused. "Dönitz and his cronies seem to know precious little about our weaponry or our tactics or our plans and yet..."

"And yet...?" Cecil prompted.

"And yet two old codgers like us who don't even have any official capacity in the goings on can sit here in our club and discuss in detail a report that an enemy Admiral made directly to his Führer scant days ago as if it were common knowledge!"

"Well... it is, you know," said Cecil, slightly baffled by what his friend was getting at.

"Yes but... Aren't you the least bit incredulous, Cecil? Should we not be just a tad less... accepting of all this intelligence that comes so readily into the public domain? Hmn?"

Frowning, Cecil appeared to consider Walter's argument carefully for a few moments, but the frown soon gave way to his customary smile.

"It seems to me, Walter, considering what we were talking about earlier that we should have a little more faith." The smile became a toothless grin stretching from ear to ear.

"How so, hmn?" Walter asked politely.

"Consider, my friend..." Cecil was a schoolmaster coaxing understanding from a slow student. "If we can acknowledge that our boffins – our scientists and our technical geniuses – have brought the modern aeroplane so far since the bi-planes of our day, not to mention other innovations like, say, radar, why then should we doubt that they have not achieved similar advances over the proficiencies of Mata Hari?"

9

HAMMAM LIF / SOUSSE, TUNIS
August 1943

At long last Harold was granted three days leave at the rest camp in Hammam Lif. Unfortunately, on his way there the front wheel of his Matchless motorcycle caught a rut in the road and threw him for a rather nasty spill. No broken bones, so far as he knew, but enough scrapes and bruises to detract from his intended and much needed respite.

An English nursing sister put him in his place when he finally made it to the rest camp. "Bloody idiot!" she admonished while applying the bandages. "We have neither the time nor the resources to look after genuine casualties without your sort!" Harold had never felt so small in his life. But he did find one occasion to smile.

Once the nurse had finished with him, he wandered about exploring the grounds and met an officer he knew who invited Harold to join him and some American acquaintances for lunch. The rest camp was a more or less intact hotel and they were seated at a table on the patio overlooking what had once been rather ornate gardens but were now mostly mud and rubble having taken the brunt of a bomb intended for the hotel. At the foot of the gardens stood the remains of a low stone wall upon which someone had written in whitewash: *"Travaillez pour la famille et la patrie!"*

"Now ain't that jus' darlin'!" drawled the senior officer at the table, an American Major whose broad accent revealed to even the uninitiated that he came from the deep south. Pointing to the whitewashed words he intoned: "Trust the Frenchies *tuh* think about *thay-at* at a time like *thee-is*."

"What do you mean?" asked the Lieutenant seated across from him, turning to look at what the Major had seen.

"Well fer gawd's sake, son," the Major complained. "You'd o' thought they could o' written somethin' more pay-triotic, or more... yew know where ah's comin' from... more, um, *upliftin'*... whut with the *war* goin' on an' all. Yew know! One o' them French Revolution things they's so proud of like 'lee-bear-*tay*, ay-gal-ee-*tay*, frah-ter-nee-*tay*' yuh know what I mean?"

"Sorry," said the Lieutenant, "I don't speak French. What *did* they write?"

"Why, look ag'in, son," replied the Major pointing once more at the words. "'T'ain't all that difficult. Just *sa-ound* it out. You'll git the sense of it."

The Lieutenant dutifully attempted to sound out the words but after a few moments he turned back to the Major shaking his head in negation. "Sorry, Major. I can't work it out."

"What it *sayys*, Lieutenant..." said the Major, looking smug and superior, "... what it *sayys* is: 'Travel in Family Parties'."

Harold did not correct the Major with the correct phrasing, which was: "Work for the family and the homeland."

The rest leave was much too brief, but it helped a little. He returned to camp at Sousse in the wee hours of Tuesday morning, August 8th, caught almost two hours of sleep, and was back on duty by 0600 hours.

Following the morning parade, where his promotion to full Captain was made official, Harold had barely sat down at his makeshift office in the back of a lorry when a soldier showed up at the tailgate. He was slim, stood about six feet tall, and somehow contrived to look absolutely immaculate. He snapped off a salute and rattled off his name and number at a parade ground decibel level.

"Sergeant Noble Milton Sparks, 29776, reporting for duty, Sir!"

The soldier's last name, Sparks, was about the only thing that penetrated Harold's exhausted mind.

"Driver?" inquired Harold as this was the role of most of the men in his Company. He could never have enough drivers. Looking up and returning the salute he immediately realized his error when he saw the Sergeant's stripes.

"No, Sir! Batman, Sir!" answered the Sergeant, still at attention and sounding very much like a Regimental Sergeant Major that Harold remembered none too fondly – the man had been thoroughly intimidating – from The Duke of York's Barracks.

"Ah," said Harold. "You have a message for me from your officer?"

"No Sir! You are my officer, Sir!"

"Oh, I..." Harold was somewhat nonplussed for a moment. "Sorry, Sergeant Sparks. No one told me... and I guess I hadn't given any thought to the matter."

"Permission to come aboard, Sir?" The Sergeant at least was not off balance.

Harold gestured his permission and as the soldier climbed into the truck he stood up and came around his tiny desk, extending his hand.

"Welcome aboard, Sergeant," Harold smiled.

Now it was the Sergeant's turn to be a little disconcerted. He had not expected the offered handshake from an officer, but he recovered quickly and returned it with a smile of his own, somewhere between pleasure and befuddlement.

"I have a vague idea of what a batman does," Harold confessed, "but I hope you can fill me in on the details."

"Not to worry, Sir! All in good time, Sir! Tea, Sir?"

Because of the *non sequitur* Harold almost missed the last bit. Almost but not entirely.

"Thank you, Sergeant. A cup of hot tea would be most welcome right now. There's a NAAFI canteen about 300 yards up that way," he pointed.

"Yes, Sir! I know, Sir!" said his new batman, removing a backpack that Harold had not even registered until now and producing from it a thermos full of steaming tea, a tin cup, a spoon, a tin can of condensed milk, and a packet of sugar.

"Sir!" The batman came to attention with the thermos and the tin cup extended at arm's length in front of him. "How do you take your tea, Sir?"

Harold couldn't hide a grin. "With milk and sugar and a little less volume please, Sergeant Sparks."

"Sir?" Sparks inquired, cocking his head slightly to one side.

"I have a headache, Sergeant. I almost always have a headache. So please keep your voice down. You don't have to whisper but please stop trying to sound like a drill sergeant on the parade square. Can you manage that, Sergeant Sparks?"

"Yes, Sir! Sorry, Sir! Your tea, Sir? It's Nobby, Sir!" the subdued batman offered contritely in a much quieter voice, coming forward with the cup of tea he had poured.

Accepting the hot tin cup Harold had once more to replay what the man had said to try to make some sense of it.

"I beg your pardon, Sergeant. Did you say the tea is 'nobby'?

"No, Sir! Me, Sir! I'm, Nobby. That's my name, Sir!" Even speaking at a normal level, he somehow managed to convey an exclamation mark every time he said 'Sir!' "If that's all right with you, Sir!"

"Splendid, Nobby," said Harold as he sipped at the life-saving brew, a little more of the tension of the headache and the worry seemingly carried away with each swallow. "Absolutely splendid."

Within days Harold came to appreciate having Nobby around. Within a month he had learned to treasure the man.

IN THE DRAWING ROOM
August 2, 1943

"The Yanks are taking it on the chin, hmn?" came Walter's slightly muffled voice, his face buried in *The Times*.

"How's that?" asked Cecil, roused from some private reverie.

"Bombing raid on a place called Ploetsi in Romania. Meant to destroy their oil refineries, it says here."

Several long seconds elapsed in silence. Finally, Cecil reached over, grasped the top of the newspaper, and slowly bent it back so that he could see Walter's face. "And...?"

"And... " The perplexed look on Walter's face elicited a low growl from his friend before he realized what he had left unsaid. "Ah, er... sorry, old chap. Yes, the thing is, you see, they were pretty badly shot up." He flapped the newspaper noisily, straightening out the crease that Cecil had put in it. "Here it is..." he said, looking up to ensure he had Cecil's attention.

"The raid involved 178 of their B-24 Liberator bombers. At last report there were 46 confirmed lost, 58 badly damaged, and 8 missing and unaccounted for."

Cecil sat back and snorted in disgust. Walter lowered his paper into his lap and looked at him, a patient, hopeful expression on his face. Cecil knew exactly what was expected of him but was having a hard time coming up with anything appropriate.

"Yes, well, you know..." he began tentatively, "at least these days we can say that *we* are bombing the enemy more often than he is bombing us." He knew it was a rather weak offering and looked sheepishly over at Walter for approbation. He could see the wheels turning.

Indeed, Walter had been fruitlessly searching his memory of recent events in the hope of being able to contribute to the counterbalancing of the hapless newspaper article. Unable to improve upon Cecil's effort, he could only respond to it.

"There is that, old chap. There is that."

At Medjez-el-Bab, May 1943

A Desert Song

10

LONDON / BRAMSHOTT – ENGLAND
August through December 1943

Frustratingly, it was not until August that Ruby finally had her Labour Exit Permit signed. For some unexplained reason they all had to return from Montreal to Toronto to be fingerprinted and have their shots. Then it was back to Montreal but not to board a ship as they had anticipated. Rather, they were given two hours to collect their baggage and were then put on another train, this one to Halifax. Once there, it was straight on-board ship, which was a dismayingly small converted banana boat. Its only armaments were an anti-aircraft gun mounted on the foredeck and a single depth charge precariously suspended from a boom over the stern.

It took them three days just to reach Newfoundland and almost a day on top of that to receive clearance before being guided in through the minefields in Saint John's harbour. Shore leave was out of the question as they were expected to join a convoy sometime within the next 72 hours. There was nothing to do but read, write letters or diaries, play bridge, stroll around the deck, and try to sleep. However, the first night in harbour the latter proved almost impossible because of the interminable rumbling and thumping of coal being loaded into the ship's bunkers.

When at last they did get under way three days later, Ruby was happy to discover that she was one of the few who had her sea legs and was therefore spared the indignity of running to the head or to the railing every few hours. Despite the ever-present fear of the dreaded U-boat wolf packs, the two-week crossing went happily without serious incident apart from a few storms that caused some of the vessels to temporarily lose contact with the convoy. The abnormally crowded quarters on board the ship were not entirely without benefit as it meant that all the Red Cross girls – strangers to one another from many different parts of Canada – were thrust together in such a manner that they had to get to know one another in short order. Ruby was surprised to learn that, other than the First Aid courses they had all been obliged to take, only two of the other girls had any nursing background. Most of her travelling companions had been recruited for their driving skills, and three were actually certified auto mechanics! She couldn't wait to write to her dad about that!

Still, getting acquainted consumed only so many hours a day. The meals were quite good. After all, the ship's galley had been provisioned in Canada where rationing was nowhere near the serious challenge it had become in Britain. (That was going to be a nasty surprise to all of them.) Unfortunately, you couldn't linger over your food drawing out the inherent pleasure of dining with convivial associates so as to kill a little more time. There were four sittings for each of the three daily meals and the sitting you attended was determined by a roster posted each evening that ensured that all the names were rotated on a regular basis. Even if you were on the list for the fourth sitting of breakfast or lunch you had to get out of the way of the kitchen staff hastily preparing for the first sitting of the next meal. If you were lucky enough to be included as a member of the fourth sitting for dinner you might be tempted to stay behind after the meal for an hour or so. But by then it would be well past midnight and everyone, regardless of which breakfast sitting they were scheduled for, was expected to be up and about not later than 0530 hours.

Getting accustomed to ordering your life according to the 24-hour hour clock that the military insisted upon was actually fun for the first few days. But again, it didn't contribute much in the way of killing time. Otherwise, there was lifeboat drill, physical training (PT) exercises, and fending off the advances of certain types who apparently were not acquainted with the phrase "an officer and a gentleman" to break the monotony.

Arriving in Liverpool they were herded aboard a train to London where they were billeted at the Canadian Red Cross Corps House, 20 Queen's Gate Terrace, and granted five days leave. Ruby took the opportunity to visit her Uncle Jack Cobbett and his wife Edie, neither of whom she had ever met, in Romford, Essex. She immediately fell in love with the couple and their small, charming cottage called Tiverton at 157 Lodge Avenue. Little did she know at the time that this address would come to hold a very special place in her heart.

Back at Corps House they shared various duties from cooking to winding bandages, preparing packages for hospitals and parcels for prisoners of war. At night, of course, on rotating shifts, it was up to the roof for fire watch duty—an always eerie and sometimes frightening experience. Yet on the rare night when the moon and stars could be seen through the usually omnipresent cloud cover, sitting up there surrounded by the utter blackness of the great city of London with only the sounds of passing vehicles and perhaps the wail of an occasional siren somewhere off in the distance, could also be strangely enchanting.

As the days passed in ones and twos, the newly arrived Canadians were given their assignments. Most of the girls Ruby had come over with were seconded to the British Red Cross to serve as ambulance or transport drivers. Before the month was out, nearly half their number had figuratively disappeared to take up their posts elsewhere but many remained at Corps House, using that as their official base. It was only another two weeks before Ruby and several other VADs with more medical experience than a quick St. John's Ambulance First Aid course were posted to various English hospitals as nurse's aides. In these settings, they had their first direct contact with the casualties of the war, both military and civilian.

The Matron of the hospital in Bramshott where Ruby and two of her younger cohorts were assigned welcomed them warmly, sincerely grateful for their presence and the much-needed extra help they offered. Many of the hospitals either had specialized wards or had been converted in their entirety to care for a specific type of injury. Loss of sight at this one, loss of hearing at that one, loss of limbs at the next. The gruesome catalogue of afflictions seemed to go on without end. Bramshott, they soon discovered, had a little bit of everything.

The Matron sat them down in her tiny office and exchanged introductions and necessary formalities over tea and biscuits, smiling and bubbling effusively all the while until she reluctantly but inescapably came to the phrase: "And now, ladies, as for your duties here..."

A series of emotions flashed across the Matron's face, but in the end she mastered them and adopted a grim, businesslike expression. She gazed steadily for a few seconds into the eyes of each of the three young women across from her.

"I fear that none of your previous experience will have prepared you for what you are going to see here," she began. "I warn you now to harden your hearts and lock your emotions away. No matter what, you must never show fear. You must never show doubt. Most difficult of all, I assure you— you must never, never show pity!" She paused to watch their reactions to her seemingly callous words and was not surprised to see the frowns and looks of confusion.

"Please understand," she continued. "If a patient here thinks you pity him, he will begin to believe that he is to be pitied. Self-pity leads rapidly to despair and despair is contagious. We cannot afford that. Is that clear?" Again, she held the eyes of each of them until she received an acknowledging nod of acquiescence then stood up abruptly. "Right then, follow me. I'll walk you 'round the wards."

It was a walk Ruby would never forget. Punctuated by the inordinately loud clicking of their own heels on the sterile terrazzo floors and broken only by the occasional groan from one of the beds, they walked beside the Matron, listening raptly to her low monotone voice murmuring the prognosis of each patient they came to. "... shrapnel still in his lungs. ... vocal chords destroyed... paralyzed from the waist down... hearing may never return... must learn to write with his left hand... never see again... never walk again... has already learned to hold a pencil with his toes... will be fitted with a plastic bag..."

Not until hours later when the initial shock and horror had abated somewhat did Ruby remember an aspect of that walking tour that she had somehow not registered at the time. She had been too overwhelmed, her senses numbed, her thoughts whirling. But now thinking back she realized that the most amazing of all the sights she had seen on that first tour of the hospital wards was the one that would sustain her. It was the smiles of the wounded patients. Those who could... those who had been awake... those whose heads were not swathed in bandages... those whose faculties were not exclusively focused on pain or dimmed by morphine... they had *smiled* at the Matron. They had *smiled* at the young women with her. Ruby smiled herself then. She remembered quite clearly now that she really thought about it—one or two of the men had even winked at her!

IN THE DRAWING ROOM
September 8, 1943

"Oh God! That's *awful!*" Walter wheezed, holding his sides and struggling with no hint of success to stop laughing.

Altogether pleased with himself, Cecil grinned back at him like the Cheshire cat.

"A *toe*hold!" Walter erupted. "We've gained a *toe*hold on Europe! Oh, Cecil... *really!*"

"Actually, my good fellow," Cecil said with genuine good humour, "one might say, you know, that we've got our jaws clenched well above the ankle... into the tender calf, so to speak!"

"Stop it, Cecil!" chortled. "I shall lose my breakfast if you keep on like this!"

Both men were clearly elated over the long-anticipated Allied invasion of continental Europe from North Africa by way of Sicily into the boot of Italy. Progress had been halting and tentative in the early going, but for the past few weeks the newspapers and the wireless had been declaring conquest after conquest, victory after victory. True the Allied advances were costing dearly—but when all was said and done they were still advances.

Italy had secretly capitulated to the Allies in Sicily on September 3rd. *Il Duce* as Mussolini had come to be called during the war years, after more than 20 years as Italy's Fascist dictator, had earlier been deposed by a vote of no confidence by the Fascist Grand Council, and King Victor Emmanuel had subsequently had him imprisoned. In September at Hitler's personal insistence, a daring raid by the German SS had succeeded in rescuing Mussolini from his security-lax jailors but for all intents and purposes the diminutive dictator – he was even shorter than Hitler – was, thereafter of no real relevance, even as a figurehead, to the ongoing conflicts.

"Terrible puns, I freely admit," said Cecil, unwilling just yet to let his captive audience of one distract him. "But not really as funny as you seem to find them, you know. No, my friend. If you wish to contemplate something that I personally assess to be much more hilarious then I pray you, consider *this*!"

He waited while Walter took a few deep breaths and was able to manifest something resembling attentiveness.

"The Italians, our erstwhile stalwart allies of the First World War, who have in this war shown themselves to be at best craven jellyfish..."

"Quite so! Quite so!" Walter interjected. They both understood that he was recalling the headline in *The Times* some weeks back vaunting the fact that more than 7,000 Italian troops had willingly surrendered to a single British Tommy near some unpronounceable place in Tunisia.

"The Italians," Cecil resumed, mildly annoyed at the interruption, "have now declared war against the Reich and propose..." It came out in a rush. "... *to fight alongside our boys!*"

20 Queen's Gate Terrace

11

FOGGIA / SAN SALVO, ITALY
December 1943

They had come out of Bizerte in mid-October, sailing to Taranto by way of Catania in Sicily. By early December, after brief stays at Bari and Termoli, they had settled in at San Salvo.

Despite the almost constant thundering of nearby artillery and bombs that permeated the air night and day and the occasional crackling outburst of small-arms fire nearby, so far Harold had experienced only one truly frightening episode since arriving in Italy. That was the night before.

It was almost 2300 hours and pitch black. He was riding his motorcycle back to San Salvo from a Court of Enquiry meeting in Foggia when a rat darted across the road in front of him and was briefly illuminated by the bike's partially shielded headlamp. Instinctively he braked to a stop. Swearing under his breath but nevertheless laughing at himself he started off again. He had not gone two feet when something unyielding struck him across the upper lip and knocked him off the motorcycle into a backward somersault.

He had been warned about this. They all had. Piano wires (of all things!) stretched across the road at roughly the height of a man's neck, designed to do precisely what it had almost done to him. If he had been going at even 20 miles an hour... Had it not been for that rat...

He let his pencil moustache grow into a bush to hide the scar.

All things considered, Harold was feeling much better. Maybe it was the climate, he thought—there were two inches of snow on the ground this morning. In any event, the malaria had not bothered him for weeks now, and the migraines were fewer and farther between. Whiskey was still hard to come by, but reasonably good wine was plentiful, and the food was decidedly better than it had been in North Africa. It was a wonderful opportunity to practice his Italian and expand his vocabulary, and there seemed to be a piano in every little inn or restaurant or hotel they encountered. Or maybe it was all thanks to Nobby, who seemed to anticipate his every need and who had proved to be a first-rate scrounger and trader. He had even managed to find some real coffee yesterday. Yes, Nobby deserved the promotion to Lieutenant that Harold had recommended. He hoped it would be approved soon.

The only really disquieting note was another letter from his mother that had come the week before. It concerned his wife, Betty, again. His mother no longer troubled herself to conceal her distress with such polite phrases as: "not behaving as she should." She wrote quite plainly and painfully.

November 2, 1943

Dearest Toddy:

> *I trust that you have by now received the cigarettes and chocolate we sent to you at about this time last month, although, as I imagine you are aware, they are nearly as rare here at home nowadays as they must be where (ever) you are. Your sister Rene and I are knitting socks for you that should be ready by the next parcel—certainly in time for Christmas.*
> *We had your letter of October 3rd in today's mail, though your subsequent letter of October 16th arrived four days ago. It is very confusing, trying to follow the sequence of events, when letters arrive out of order! It is also disconcerting, while admittedly, a bit of a novelty, to read letters from which words have been cut*

out with a razor blade! Your father tells me that this is "in the interests of National Security." In any event, your father and I are delighted to know that you are keeping well. (Any recurrence of the malaria? You will tell us, won't you, Toddy?)

No doubt you will share our pride to know that Chicks is still putting her driving skills to work for the cause, driving ambulances in London after and, I believe it Toddy, even during the bombing. (Happily, they don't come nearly as frequently as they used to.) Over supper, she has recounted numerous adventures of dodging bomb craters and even tumbling buildings, yet she is always most modest about her accomplishments. She and you are so much alike, Toddy!

Rene is continuing to do her part, too, volunteering her time and her magnificent voice to entertaining the troops, who are mostly Americans nowadays. She confides, frequently, that she devoutly wishes you were still here to accompany her. While she has not entirely forgone the supper clubs, she now even sings in the open-air band stands of the parks. Her major concern is that her voice is not strong enough for the venue.

But now, my dear Toddy, I am afraid that I can put it off no longer. The real reason why I am writing this letter. Brace yourself, my dear, for I have evil tidings to impart. Please forgive me. Your father wanted to wait until "all this business" (the war,) was over, but I felt, as your mother, I could not allow this to go on without your knowledge.

Your Betty has been unfaithful to you.

I refused to believe the rumours at first, but several close friends have confirmed them.

Toddy dear, I am so sorry. I shall take no overt action until I have heard back from you.

Your loving mother,

Violet

P.S. Your father sends his best.

———⋄⊰⊱⋄———

Not. Bloody. Good. At-oll!

Harold was heartbroken. He knew, of course, that some of the wives of men who had been away from them for a prolonged period were unfaithful. In the past year alone, he had personally recommended or endorsed compassionate leave for several men in his own Company for just such a reason. But he had never even dreamed that it could happen to him.

It took four days and four almost sleepless nights of soul-searching before he could bring himself to write to his mother. He wrote that he would request permission for home leave and would try to get back to England as soon as possible. He would talk with Betty and try to understand her side of the story before coming to any final decision.

As it turned out, however, he never got his home leave, and his mother did not in fact wait to hear from him before taking overt action.

It was information from Harold's sister, Chicks, that precipitated events. Her fiancé, Kent, (they had become engaged three months earlier) worked at the War Department, as did Betty. One evening shortly after Violet had written to tell Harold of Betty's infidelity, Chicks was confiding in Kent how unhappy she was on her brother's behalf when he interrupted her.

"I'm afraid it's even worse than you think, my love," he told her.

"Whatever do you mean?" she asked.

"I wish I were not the one to tell you this but..." he looked away, unable to continue.

"Kent, darling, what is it? You must tell me!"

With difficulty he managed to look at her again. When he eventually found his voice, the words came out in a torrent.

"Your sister-in-law was arrested this morning on a charge of suspected treason. Not only has she been sleeping around, she's been sleeping with people whom the War Department suspect to be spies!"

"Oh, dear God!" Chicks exclaimed. "Poor, poor Toddy!"

The moment Chicks informed her mother of this development, Violet took Charlie in tow. Together they swallowed their pride, mastered their shame, and, acting on their son's behalf, engaged a solicitor to sue for divorce. Betty was in no position to contest the suit. The divorce was granted—"wronged husband in absentia, loyally serving in His Majesty's forces overseas," the Magistrate took pains to emphasize in what must have been a record short time even with a war going on.

Harold learned of all this a few weeks later when his Commanding Officer, Major Stoville, called him in to refuse for the fifth time his request for home leave on compassionate grounds.

San Salvo was still some distance from the front and at first it appeared they had little more to worry about than putting in order what the advance Allied troops had left behind and, more urgently, bringing up more men and supplies. Then the looting and stealing began.

Individuals, small groups or even gangs of 15 or 20 Italians – presumably deserters, as most still wore at least the remnants of uniforms – were pilfering anything they could get their hands on. They almost always acted under the cover of darkness or occasionally, when the Allies were under fire, in daylight. When it became known that they would and often did kill to get what they wanted, the order went out to use all necessary force in self-defense. And for the first time since returning to duty with the RASC, it was under these circumstances that Harold had his first opportunity to shoot back at the enemy.

"More tea, Sir?" Nobby prompted from the depths of the lorry's interior where he had set up a little Primus stove beside Harold's shaving gear. They were en route to Termoli for yet another Court of Enquiry where Harold, the OC had informed him upon his return, was to give evidence at 1100 hours this morning. It involved one of his drivers who had been sent down for that ubiquitous charge, 'conduct prejudicial to good order and military discipline'.

They had pulled off the road for a quick bite of breakfast. Harold had managed only 90 minutes' sleep before setting out again and it was still dark. The sole source of light was a kerosene lantern, which Harold had set on his makeshift desk in an attempt to review his notes prior to the Court of Enquiry.

"Dare!" came the command in Italian out of the blackness behind the lorry. "You give!" There was a pause. "You give, you live!"

With a calm he had not known he possessed, Harold reached out and quickly turned down the wick in the kerosene lamp until it was extinguished.

"Get down, Nobby," Harold said quietly as he stood and moved to his left.

The Sergeant obeyed with alacrity, which was fortunate for at that moment three shots were fired into the interior of the lorry.

Harold had meanwhile retrieved his .45 Colt automatic pistol from his kit, which Nobby had set on the bench running along the side of the lorry's bed. Having seen the flashes from the rifles his three assailants carried, Harold had a good idea of where they stood—about 15 feet behind the tailgate, arrayed across the ditch, which meant that the one in the middle was roughly two feet below the other two. His pistol's clip held nine rounds. Before they could fire again, he did.

To Nobby's ears there were not nine separate shots only one prolonged one. In the silence that ensued he watched his officer calmly re-light the kerosene lamp, eject the spent clip from his pistol, and replace it with a full one. He picked up the lamp, walked to the tailgate, and climbed down. Inspired by the Captain's example, Nobby rose to his feet and advanced a pace or two.

In the light that spilled from the lamp, he watched Captain Harold Stanley Lawes – *his* officer – collect the rifles, pistols, knives, and grenades from the would-be robbers. As the Captain stooped with his lamp over each of the fallen men to gather their arms, Nobby saw evidence of their wounds.

All had fallen backward from the impact of the bullets. From Nobby's vantage-point the man on the left had clearly been hit at least twice, once in the right shoulder and once in the heart. Blood was issuing from the temple, chest, and groin of the man in the centre. The one on the right was face down, evidently having been spun around by the impact of one of the bullets. The Captain cautiously turned him over with the toe of his boot. Nobby gasped and closed his eyes to shut out the gruesome sight. The man had no face left.

"Lend a hand, will you, Sergeant?"

At the sound of the Captain's voice Nobby opened his eyes. The Captain had set the lantern on the edge of the tailboard and was endeavoring to push the rifles and other collected armaments onto the flatbed. Nobby came forward in a daze and bent to help his officer with the task.

No bloody good, Nobby," Harold mouthed. "No bloody good at-oll!"

It was then with the lamplight almost full in Harold's face that Nobby saw the tears.

"Oh, Sir!" he exclaimed, tears rapidly filling his own eyes. "Oh, Sir!"

IN THE DRAWING ROOM
December 2, 1943

"What do you suppose they talk about at those meetings, hmn?" Walter's queried out loud, inviting speculation from himself as much as from Cecil. But, as usual, it was the latter who was first off the mark.

"I suspect nothing more than a good old-fashioned chin wag, you know," said Cecil. "Like friends who have not seen one another for a while catching up on everything that's been happening to each of them in the interval. Asking after one another's health and that sort of thing."

"Do you really think it's that prosaic?" a dubious Walter asked.

"Not entirely perhaps but... in essence, yes, I do," Cecil affirmed.

Carefully removing the linen napkin from beneath his saucer, he rolled it tightly into a long tube. He stood up, traversed the short distance to the sofa that sat facing their habitual spot in the drawing room, and centering himself, sat down with knees widely splayed. Puffing ostentatiously on his napkin-cigar, he launched into a parody of what he imagined the Big Three summit conferences might sound like.

"Ahemm!" he began, as gutturally as his natural tenor would permit. "And how is the war going from your perspective, Mr. Roosevelt? Are your Generals happy?" He slid to his right on the smooth leather sofa, drew his knees together and cupped one hand on top of the other just below his chin, the rolled-up napkin in the bottom hand now curved like the top of a walking stick or cane.

"I am not displeased..." 'Roosevelt' responded, trying to sound as if he had a bad chest cold, each syllable carefully enunciated as if in time to a slow metronome "... with the progress of the war, Mr. Churchill. Thank you for asking. As for the Generals, well, I have no need to tell you I am sure that some of them can act like spoiled children at times. I believe you have one or two of that ilk in your own little family."

"Quite so, Mr. Roosevelt," the cigar-chomping British Prime Minister acknowledged from the centre of the sofa.

"Ahemm!" he growled, turning to his left. "And what of you, Mr. Stalin? Your Generals, it would seem, have much to be proud of." Cecil slid to his left and began tugging at one side of his upper lip as if stroking a moustache.

"Is very true, Meester Church-hill. We have managed to stem de flow..." Two quick bounces delivered Cecil to the far end of the sofa.

"More like turned the tide, I should say, Mr. Stalin!" Bounce, bounce to the opposite end. Cecil extended his left leg and leaned well forward as if peering around the imaginary Mr. Churchill at the illusory Mr. Roosevelt.

"Gra-cious of you to say so, Mr. Roosa-velt. Now if you gentlemen would do *your* part and invade Europe from de west..."

Neither Cecil nor Walter realized just how close to the mark that little bit of theatre would actually come.

12

AT SEA

January 1944

They left Bramshott on the night of January 12, 29 of them, all with full kit, packed like sardines into the backs of two trucks. Ruby was by far the tiniest woman in the group and several of her companions remarked on whether she would even be able to lift her pack let alone keep up with the rest as they climbed in and out of the trucks. They told her she looked like an overstuffed duffel bag with a bedroll on top, a haversack hanging from one side, a steel helmet from the other, and two 'cartoon feet' (she wore a size five) poking out below.

"So, what's a little curvature of the spine and a couple of dislocated ribs to complain about?" she quipped. She really *had* dislocated two ribs, but she wasn't about to tell anyone. This was the beginning of her big adventure!

They had been serving in England for four months. They endured an hour's wait at the tiny station in Liphook, sitting on the only things that resembled seats – aromatic fish crates – before the train arrived. They piled in six to a compartment and, after struggling to stow their gear, lit up the cigarettes. Hungry, they knew they would have to make do with chocolate bars until they changed trains at... somebody said it was Woking, but that didn't make a lot of sense. Did it?

Another long wait, this time with no place to sit except the floor. The second train was better, however—only four to a compartment. They were curling up as best they could with the intention of getting some sleep when one of the girls stuck her head into the compartment and said something about food, so they got up and went looking. Munching on sandwiches and cake they watched the sun rise before returning to their compartment to try to get some much-needed sleep.

They stopped in what looked like the middle of a farmer's field for tea, served from the back of a lorry. Hot tea. It was a godsend. They lined up with their mugs like a bunch of starving beggars in a bread line. Perpetual rain dripping into their mugs did nothing to detract from the pleasure of the rich, hot beverage. Then it was back onto the train and away. Within moments, they had visitors: a tall, gangly major, obviously British but whose insignia Ruby didn't recognize; a doctor and a dentist, both sporting Captain's pips, who had lectured to the group some weeks back; and a fourth man not in uniform. They crowded into the women's compartment. They were drunk, they were loud, and they sang off key, but they brought and shared whiskey and chocolate.

The next morning, after too little sleep, they struggled into their uniforms, swearing that someone had filled them with bricks. They debarked from the train to a chorus of wolf-whistles and good-humoured catcalls and found themselves on a short route march towards the ship.

No banana boat this time, they were pleased to see. Who ever heard of a banana boat with 11-inch guns?

Ruby and her companions brought up the rear. They felt like refugees.

Identification papers, march two steps, stop, march two steps more, stop. Disney should have seen us. We had the seven dwarfs beat by a mile. Twenty-nine of us and each one doing an imitation of Dopey.

For nine of the eleven days they had been at sea they had been tossed about like toy boats in a bathtub during an earthquake. From day one, as had been the case with their Atlantic crossing back in August, they had been ordered to sleep fully dressed including their boots. Their days since had been filled with more lifeboat drills and more PT sessions, (the only real novelty being lectures on gases), strolling around the deck, endless rounds of bridge, and mounting fear.

Twice they had lost contact with the rest of the convoy for several hours—hours that seemed like days. Seven or eight times they listened and watched and waited anxiously for airplanes passing overhead to be identified. They had altered course so many times that Ruby had lost all sense of direction. She was certain, however, that they were headed for North Africa. That's what it said on the Allied Force Permit she had been issued back on the first of the month. But, of course, ludicrous as it seemed she was not permitted to say so, even to her fellow passengers.

That morning shortly after breakfast the convoy had come within sight of land – Africa they were told, (ah hah!) – and mercifully the sea was finally almost calm. Perversely, that was the *only* thing that was calm just now.

Twenty minutes prior, the horn had sounded telling them to put on their life jackets followed by the most infuriating of orders: "Stand by!" Dozens of flaming canisters floated on the water setting up their smoke screen. Every time one of their four escort ships dropped a depth charge the whole ship would shudder, and they could feel the vibrations of the explosion right through the deck and the thick soles of their boots. At least two airplanes could be heard but the question hung in the air... *"Whose side are they on?"*

"Remind me to tell the Matron," Ruby said to no one in particular. "This Mediterranean cruise isn't exactly what it was cracked up to be by the travel agents back home."

Four endless hours later they emerged from the smoke screen and the all-clear was sounded. When they looked around, however, they realized that there were five fewer ships in their convoy. It was not until late that evening, speculation having run rampant, that someone finally informed them that the departure of those five ships was planned as they were going to a different destination.

As darkness fell, the southeastern horizon sparkled with the lights of unidentified African cities. One of the crew said: "That there's Tangiers."

"Not long now," said one of his mates.

"Not long for what?" asked Ruby.

"Gibraltar," he explained. "Should be able to see the lights within the hour." It was indeed a wondrous sight.

It was like a fairyland. On our right the cities lit up like little carnivals. On the left a hospital ship, blazing with white, green, and red lights, and all around us little sail and paddle boats with small torches flaring in the darkness.

For the next two days they hugged the coastline of North Africa, now more or less under Allied control. They passed *"tall, shaggy mountains varying in colour from dull gray to a hazy shade of purple; cozy little settlements nestled in among the hills, looking so very peaceful and secure. The deep, deep blue of the Mediterranean, with its many white caps that looked so much like lace ruffles on a blue dress. And a school of porpoises gracefully riding the waves."*

On January 24th they had a repeat of the scare with the smoke screen but this time no depth charges. On the 25th, they passed Bizerte then Sicily. The temperature dropped and the seas turned rough again. Several of the passengers were seasick.

Early on the morning of the 26th they spotted the beautiful Isle of Capri, and ahead, Mount Vesuvius and Naples. There were ships everywhere crisscrossing in front of and behind them. Slowly they glided into the harbour, wondering what lay ahead. Strangely, most felt a certain sense of loss at the notion of leaving the ship despite their less than salutary experience aboard her. Perhaps in part it was because they realized that they would likely be split up and might never see one another again.

13

ITALY

February 1944

On the night of January 27ᵗʰ, along with five of the original 29 nursing sisters who had left England together, (the remainder, as they had feared, having been split up and sent off to various other destinations) Ruby travelled by foot and truck to a staging area near Caserta, about 25 miles north of Naples. The passes through the Apennines had been declared impassable, so Ruby and her mates found themselves with a few days of nothing-to-do and nowhere-to-go on their hands.

"Nowhere to go? You must be joking!" Ruby protested. Within two days she had been granted permission and organized the transportation for four of them to take a day trip back into Naples. A very exotic part of that great adventure she had been dreaming of back in Hamilton was close by and Napoli's beckoning call was like the song of a siren.

They didn't have an official guide or even a city map, but their driver, a jovial young Corporal from the Royal Canadian Artillery, seemed to know his way around well enough. The most startling revelation was that so much beauty had survived the German demolition efforts and the Allied bombings. Ornate statues of saints and mythical beasts – too many to count – mounted on pedestals or atop buildings drew their attention at virtually every street corner. They "oohed" and "ahwed" at the brilliantly coloured frescoes on the walls of the Real Teatro di San Carlo. The Cupola di San Francesco, towering above the long curving lines of pillars, humbled them almost as much as Vesuvius.

A late lunch taken *al fresco* at a tiny café on the Via Santa Brigida should have been delicious. But to look up from the plate and see a young mother sitting on the curb picking lice out of her child's hair had a way of numbing the taste buds.

For Ruby, the highlight of the day was a visit to the Opera House. In the late hours of the afternoon it was almost empty and perhaps the relative quiet helped to enhance the splendour of the magnificent decor. They were able to go anywhere they wanted to—on stage, backstage, and eventually into the box seats.

It was a strange feeling. Not... uncomfortable exactly but... odd. To be sitting there in khaki battle dress and army boots and realize that not so long ago some of the best dressed women in the world sat in these same box seats gowned in silks and ermines and jewels.

Holidays are never long enough. At least in the coming days Ruby and three of her chums could reflect on the glories they had seen in the ancient city of Naples as they made their way over the Apennines and settled in to assume their duties with No. 1 Canadian General Hospital in Barletta on the Adriatic coast.

Even her experience at the hospital in Bramshott had not prepared her for this. Many of the injuries she had seen there were no less grievous, but in Bramshott the wounds had already been treated and dressed in clean bandages and plaster casts. Everything from the bed linens to the floors had looked and smelled antiseptic. Not so here.

Here 'sterile' was a relative term. The operating theatres retained that pristine state for all of two minutes after the first casualties were brought in. Blood, mud, human excrement, and other unidentifiable filth dropped from stretchers, boots, and clothing as the patients were delivered, quickly dispelling any thought or hope of maintaining a truly sterile environment. It went on and on, interminable hour after interminable hour. And still they came. There were too many! They came too fast! This was chaos!

Yet, there was order. Even the greenest among them – and Ruby certainly counted herself one of those – managed to do what was required, what they had been trained to do. She was a Registered Nurse and even in civilian life she had seen and treated victims of accidents and violence. She had dealt with compound fractures, multiple lacerations, even severed fingers. In the hospital at Bramshott, she had seen and helped to treat the effects, the aftermath, of horrific war-wounds. But she had never seen or even imagined, in her worst nightmares, the unspeakable carnage to human flesh to which she was now a first-hand witness.

How could there possibly be so much blood?

She was there, she reminded herself, because she had volunteered to serve as a Red Cross Welfare Officer. Perhaps she should be grateful that one of the services had *not* taken her on as a nursing sister as she had originally hoped.

During a brief lull in the activity she made her way back out to the receiving area. She walked up and down the lines of those who were waiting patiently (and, God love them, for the most part without complaint) for medical attention. Her official responsibilities were not that complex. Offer a few words of comfort, pass out cigarettes while the medical officers (MO) performed their secondary triage—the primary triage having been rendered at a casualty clearing station (CCS) closer to the front. Unofficially, it was not that easy.

"You watch one die... and bite your lip so as not to cry. You walk on to the next with a wisecrack ready."

"Just to hear your voice—a voice from home! They would smile... or try to."

"It's good for a girl's ego to overhear a Canadian boy say to a Tommy or an Aussie next to him: 'That's one of our *girls... not bad, eh?'"*

Ruby quickly realized that adjustments to being in the field were not confined to her duties at the hospital. Sharing with five other girls a room not much bigger than the one she had had to herself in her parents' home demanded a lot of patience and tolerance from all concerned. It wasn't so difficult to remember to shake out the bed clothes and take a liberal dusting of Keating's Powder for Fleas before turning in. They still woke up with bites in places they didn't really want to tell anyone about, but shudder to think how bad it might have been without those simple precautions. And she could never quite get used to picking the still-wriggling wasps out of the jam or marmalade that she spread on her bread at breakfast.

IN THE DRAWING ROOM
January 1, 1944

"And a damn fine job it was, too!" Cecil proclaimed, thumping his knee for emphasis.

"Hear, hear!" Walter agreed. "It's a pity that Canada is not a more populous country. We could do with a great many more like these lads, hmn?" He returned his attention to his newspaper. "Ortona, it's called, on the Adriatic coast."

"Yes, yes, I've read the article," said Cecil impatiently. "Have you gotten to the part that tells how they advanced from house to house by..."

"'By dynamiting holes in the walls and crawling through, so as to avoid being exposed to enemy sniper fire,'" Walter finished for him, reading directly from the newspaper. "Ingenious, wouldn't you agree? Hmn?"

"You know, Walter," smiled Cecil, "I believe that is an even more appropriate choice of adjective than the one the columnist used... although, I suppose 'resourceful' isn't too bad, either."

"'...an important and heavily defended enemy defensive line has thus been breached...'" read Walter.

"Earlier in the article, he said it was called The Gustav Line,'" Cecil interrupted.

"Trouble is, old chap," said Walter, frowning, "he says that the most formidable part of The Gustav Line, around... um, let me see... around a place called Monte Cassino, is still firmly entrenched. What's more, they've got another, even stronger defensive line, already established, just a few miles north."

"I know," Cecil frowned back at him. "That one's called The Hitler Line. Imagine how committed they will be to defend a line with a name like that!"

Walter looked at his friend with a twinkle in his eyes. "True, Cecil, true. On the other hand... " He paused, waiting.

After a moment of reflection, Cecil's face lit up. "Imagine how a name like that will inspire our boys to want to destroy it!"

No. 3022

ALLIED FORCE PERMIT

The bearer of this permit has the permission of the Commanding General Allied Forces to enter the Zone of the Allied Forces in

NORTH AFRICA

Le titulaire est autorisé d'entrer dans la Zone de l'Armée Alliée en

NORTH AFRICA

This permit must be produced when required together with the bearer's identity document.
Ce permis doit être presente à toute demande avec le document d'identité du titulaire.

Allied Force Permit (Front)

Issued by / Emis par .... LONDON
Date .... 4 JAN 1944

Valid from / Validité du } 4.1.44 until / au } 4.6.44

Destination NORTH AFRICA
UNDER ORDERS OF CANADIAN
Object of Journey } RED CROSS SOCIETY

Rank FIRST AID NURSE

Full name of Bearer / Prénom et nom du Titulaire } RUBY GEORGINA GOBBETT

Nationality / Nationalité } BRITISH
CANADIAN

Number and Type of Identity Document } PASSPORT 345343
CANADIAN RED

Ministry or Dept. supporting journey } CROSS SOCIETY

Signature { of Bearer / du Titulaire }

Issuing Officer's Signature, Rank and Appointment

For Comndg.-General, A.F.H.Q.

Endorsements

(B43/344) 10000 8/43 W.O.P. 13952 T.S. 6402

Allied Force Permit (Back)

PART 3

FUGUE

14

BARLETTA, ITALY

Early March 1944

Ruby was sitting on the edge of her bed in the second-floor hotel room where they had been billeted. She was crying and had been doing so for almost an hour now. Catherine Young, her 'new best friend' and current roommate (only two to a room now and in what had once been a very posh hotel—much had improved since they first arrived) tried to console her, plying her with straight rye whiskey.

In some ways they were an unlikely pairing. Catherine was over six feet tall. Whenever they were seen together, diminutive Ruby and towering Catherine, they inevitably attracted the appellation Mutt and Jeff. Officially still CRCC Welfare Officers, they were both, in fact, Registered Nurses and often quietly and unofficially found themselves conscripted into fulfilling the role of a nursing sister.

In her hands Ruby held a cable from the War Office informing her that her young brother, Jack, was missing and presumed dead. The Lancaster Bomber in which 21-year-old Sergeant John Cobbett of the RCAF had served as tail gunner had been shot down over Berlin on January 3rd. This terrible news had only now caught up with her more than a month after the fact.

"Pull yourself together, love," urged Catherine as sounds from a large gathering of assorted ranks and disciplines drifted up from the hotel lobby. There was nothing unusual in this – the customary cacophony of voices in conversation or song, the thick haze of smoke, the tinkle of glasses – all were common to any such gathering. Ruby knew she shouldn't be annoyed by it but for some reason she was.

She struggled to pull her emotions under control. Normally, she was their mistress. She had to be. There was simply too much pain and suffering and the strained emotions of others to cope with every day for her to not keep her own emotions in check. My God, all those wounded and dying men and women and children, soldiers and civilians alike, (some of the soldiers were mere boys) to whom she and her coworkers ministered every day! *"Think about their suffering!"* she tried to tell herself. *"I'm being selfish and irrational. They don't know I'm sitting here with this damned cable."*

Angry with herself for allowing this unaccustomed lapse of self-control, she let her head fall forward and squeezed her eyes shut in a vain effort to stem the tears. She felt Catherine's hand on her shoulder and wiped ineffectually at her cheeks with a crumpled handkerchief trying to force a smile. Catherine attempted to push a glass of rye into her hands and take the cable away.

"Thanks, old girl," Ruby managed, an unusual term of endearment as Catherine was five years younger. "I'm all right now. I wonder if Mom and Dad know yet?"

Carefully she folded the cable, placed it inside a notebook and, setting the notebook aside, accepted the glass of rye from her friend. She uttered a deep, prolonged sigh followed by a shudder and took a gulp, the tears gradually diminishing as the sweet liquor burned in the back of her throat and down her esophagus into her belly.

"See?" she said, sitting up straight and affecting an air of bravado. She looked at Catherine and raised her glass in salute. "I'm a lot tougher than I look," she said without conviction.

Ruby brought the glass to her lips once more but before she could take a sip her eyes suddenly opened wide in a look of profound surprise. Almost immediately, despite her resolve, the tears started flowing again and quickly degenerated into racking sobs.

Shaking her head and feeling useless, Catherine came back to Ruby's side. She was just reaching out a comforting hand when Ruby's head snapped up. Catherine started. Clearly her distraught friend was once more in control of herself but Catherine did not at first know whether to feel relief or dismay, for the look now on her friend's normally composed face was not one she had ever seen before and it was frightening. This was not the look of loss and grief that she had been watching compassionately and patiently for the past hour. This was a look of dire menace.

"What..." mumbled Catherine as soon as she got a grip on herself, "What is it? What's the matter?"

"*Now* I understand why I couldn't stop my damn crying," Ruby almost spat the words.

She didn't look at Catherine but rather glared at the floor as if she could see right through it into the hotel lobby below where a motley collection of off-duty soldiers, sailors, medical personnel, and who-knew-what were congregated.

"What? You do?" stammered poor Catherine. "Ruby, for goodness' sake, what is it?"

Ruby's glare turned toward Catherine, its inherent vehemence undiminished. She stamped her size-five boot on the floor with such force that the bottle of rye on the side table clinked against the glasses beside it.

"Catherine, my friend," she intoned in a low almost masculine rumble that belied her tiny feminine frame. "Please, go downstairs and tell that bastard to *get off the piano!*"

Catherine was completely at a loss. She regarded her friend closely, concerned that the shock of learning of her brother's death had been too much for her on top of all the horrors they had to deal with every day in the casualty clearing stations and base hospital. Ruby would not be the first non-combatant in this gruesome war whose sanity was sorely tested nor indeed broken, and yet Catherine knew Ruby possessed a strength of character and will surpassing almost any of the many others with whom she had served. It was one of the reasons she had been drawn to Ruby in the first place. It was comforting and reassuring to have that kind of strength so close at hand. So steadfast, so dependable; dear, diminutive Ruby was always there when you needed her, with a joke or some homespun wisdom or just her competence in the operating room. This reversal of roles was entirely unanticipated.

"Catherine!" Ruby drew her from her reverie, "Just *listen!*"

Catherine, still somewhat confounded, listened. And then it hit her. "Well, I'll be blued and tattooed!" she exclaimed, using one of her more infrequent if not more colourful expressions, tears returning to her own eyes again. "Oh, you poor dear!" she sniffled, "Of course! I understand!" She hurried from the room leaving Ruby alone with her thoughts.

From below in the hotel lobby for the umpteenth time that evening came the strains of a small makeshift orchestra, eagerly busking along with the pianist, playing one of the most popular tunes of the day. It was carried on voices coloured by all the emotions engendered in men and women from a thousand varied backgrounds, a hundred different cultures, and one common thread.

The piano player, cigarette dangling from the corner of his lower lip, was just trying to relax a little. His Company had at long last been pulled out of the line for a well-deserved respite, and he had come down to the hotel bar this evening to have a few drinks and unwind. He was known to many in attendance so naturally, unavoidably, but also quite willingly he had allowed himself to be cajoled into providing the evening's entertainment. He had wished nothing more than to accommodate and hopefully please his genuinely appreciative audience, so he had played the tune over and over each time they had called for it. Members of the impromptu orchestra were only too delighted to accompany whatever he chose to play. That tune was, "We'll meet Again."

And so it was, although somewhat indirectly, that "Mr. and Mrs. Rat" first became acquainted with one another.

"Sir! You were only doing your bit as you always do to help the lads unwind a little."

"I know that, Nobby," said Harold. "But can you imagine what that poor woman must have been going through?"

"Indeed, Sir! And I am full of sympathy," Nobby intoned with sincerity. "But to suggest that you stop playing altogether... *Really*, Sir!"

"The lady was only delivering a message, Nobby, and she relented as soon as she had said it," Harold sighed. "In the end she asked only that I not play that particular piece again."

"And so you did not, Sir! Therefore, I cannot comprehend your continuing discomfiture over the matter."

"They'll be expecting me to play again tonight. They'll be asking for "We'll Meet Again" and she's still there. To many of them the song expresses a hope, a promise, a reason to keep on. To her it's a cruel reminder of a loved one lost."

He sighed as deeply as Nobby had ever heard his Captain sigh.

"It's no bloody good, Nobby. Perhaps... I should simply stay away for the evening."

Of course, he did not, *could* not stay away from his beloved piano and from the simple joy of giving that his playing permitted him. This was one of his few releases from the horror that surrounded them all.

Of course, there were many repeated requests for "We'll Meet Again" and for a long while he was able to avoid playing that particular piece as there were always other tunes being called for: "Underneath the Arches," "You'll Never Know," "There, I've Said It Again," "Rum and Coca Cola," "Knocked 'em in the Old Kent Road," "A Foggy Night in London Town." The possible requests – and he consoled himself that he now had more than 400 popular pieces in his repertoire – were even more numerous than the throng of people gathered in the hotel bar.

Of course, he could not evade the inevitable for the entire evening. Particularly when just as he was finishing "White Cliffs of Dover" and preparing to launch into "I've Got a Lovely Bunch of Coconuts," a petite, pert, shapely, ash-blond Lieutenant in the uniform of the Canadian Red Cross Corps appeared at his side with a brimming glass of scotch in each hand, one extended toward Harold and said: "I owe you one."

For the first time in almost two hours he actually stopped playing. He couldn't tear his eyes away from hers which, while dry, were filled with so much emotion that they held him spellbound.

"To life!" she toasted, pushing the glass of scotch into his hand. She looked at him over the brim of her own. "To life! And to you, Captain, and to those like you. You help to give us... *all* of us... some hope for better times."

She raised her glass and took a large swallow of the potent liquor. Uncomprehending, he followed suit, still unable to look away from those scintillating blue eyes.

"Would you play something for me?" she asked, her oh, so beautiful eyes misting even more. "Would you please play, 'We'll Meet Again'?"

Finally, Harold blinked. "I... uh..." he muttered, looking into his glass.

"*I'm* the one who sent Catherine to you last night asking you to stop playing," she said, so softly that Harold had to lean forward to hear her clearly. "I'm the one who could not even think of anyone else's grief but her own." Ruby sighed deeply and took another large gulp of scotch. How she managed to avoid gagging was a wonder.

Harold was out of his depth. Here was a woman in despair, despair as deep or deeper than any he had himself experienced – and his own experiences of the war were by no means trivial – who was asking him to do something that he knew would bring her pain.

"*Would you please play 'We'll Meet Again'?*"

"Why..." he stammered. "Are you sure...?"

"For them," Ruby indicated with a glance over her right shoulder toward the long bar and the congregation of assorted ranks and nationalities, all of them taken up with small talk, alcohol, cigarettes, and the unspoken but cherished respite from duty. "And for me, too."

She set her now empty glass on the piano. "I don't know if I'll ever heal from the wound that I feel in my heart from the loss of my brother. But I do know that I am needed here. And I know that I'm not the only one who is needed. We all are. But most especially people like *you* are needed, Captain."

She reached out and gently placed her hand on his forearm.

"Your music is a tonic, a... a pain killer. It's from another time and place and it helps us..." She took a deep breath, composing herself. "It's a lovely song, 'We'll Meet Again.' Full of all the very real and very desperate wishes and fears of everyone in this room and thousands more besides. I had no right to ask you to stop, it's just that..."

"Oh, but you had *every* right," Harold interrupted. "Your friend... Catherine?... she explained everything to me."

Harold drained his own glass and set it beside the other on the piano. "There are many popular tunes. I don't *have* to play that one."

"I *want* you to play it," Ruby said, calmly. "My brother Jack and I *will* meet again. I have every confidence in God," she vowed, tears threatening.

"Sit," he invited, leaning over and pulling a nearby, temporarily empty chair, up to the piano with his right hand and shifting a little to his left. She hesitated only for a moment then did so.

For 30 minutes or more, with Ruby seated at his side, he played nothing but boisterous and rollicking tunes that had even the quietest of the gathering singing along, tapping their feet, or clapping in rhythm. Ruby herself finally joined in the singing – and the applause – and as each rousing chorus ended Harold launched into the next.

With the final strains of "Beer Barrel Polka" fading into the overriding background noise of the conversation, the clinking of glasses and the shuffling of feet, Harold turned to look at Ruby. He put his right hand on her forearm and said quietly: "For you, dear one." And then he played.

He played "We'll Meet Again," and Ruby wept as dozens of voices around her were raised in song. Then he played selections from the score of "The Desert Song," which he had played to accompany the singing of his eldest sister, Irene, before the war. There were fewer voices joining in this time – sometimes only one or two – but all of those gathered about were quietly attentive. He followed this with Chopin's "Black Key" *étude* and the room fell utterly silent. The bass chords were still reverberating when he launched into Chopin's "Fantaisie-Impromptu," swiftly followed by Liszt's "La Campanella," and the entire company was held enraptured.

When he finally stopped playing there was a resounding cheer and much clapping and shouts of "Bravo!" and "Encore!" which continued for several minutes. Apart from "We'll Meet Again," no one had requested any of the pieces he had played since and indeed Harold had not played any of them or anything *like* them since before the war. With the crowd almost roaring about them he turned and looked at the young woman seated beside him.

"I'm Harold," he said quietly. "Harold Lawes."

"Harold," she repeated. "That's my father's name."

"What's your name, dear one?"

"Ruby... Ruby Cobbett," she answered, returning his frank gaze. "And, thank you!"

"Not at all," he smiled. "Now I owe *you* one!"

IN THE DRAWING ROOM
March 15, 1944

"A tough nut, Walter. This blasted Monte Cassino – and I do mean *blasted* – you've read the article?" Cecil paused, teacup halfway to his mouth, and looked up.

"Nothing much left of the monastery but a pile of rubble, he claims," Walter concurred. "Apparently, it must have seemed like a good idea at the time... shelling and bombing it, I mean, before sending the ground troops back in."

"I can certainly understand that," Cecil nodded. "But now, they wish they hadn't because the rubble and craters caused by the bombardment are providing Jerry with even better cover than he had before! It's so bad we can't even get our tanks through it to support the infantry!"

"Did you read the sidebar?" asked Walter.

"No, what does it say?"

"Well, evidently the usual collection of 'Generals-by-hindsight' are suggesting that the Germans were not even *in* the monastery building itself, not wanting to draw fire to an historical landmark."

"Oh, hell's bells," cursed Cecil. "That story's just unlikely enough to be true!"

15

BARLETTA, ITALY

Late March 1944

"Have you always had a mustache?" she asked him over breakfast the next morning.

"Well, I've let it grow recently," he grinned. "Why do you ask?"

"It tickles," she offered quietly, glancing down at her half-finished meal and trying with a surprising degree of success to look demure. "Would you consider shaving it off?"

Harold recounted his near miss with the piano wire and the rat running across the road and explained how he had let his piano moustache grow out to hide the ugly gash in his upper lip.

"A *rat*!" she exclaimed rather too loudly.

"That's right, deary!" chimed in one of the English nursing sisters at the next table who had only overheard Ruby's exclamation. She was a large, plump woman with a perfectly round face. "You've got yourself a proper Rat there!"

"I beg your pardon!" said Ruby, sitting bolt upright and fixing the woman with an icy stare. Not taken aback in the least the buxom English woman continued.

"A *genuine* Rat, deary. Not one o' them as lays false claim to the name, like them Johnny-come-lately Yanks." She turned to Harold beaming and gave him a big wink with a tilt of her head. "Good on you, Mister Rat!"

she concluded, returning her attention completely to her breakfast tray as if nothing untoward had occurred.

Ruby wasn't about to let this apparently callous insult to her breakfast companion and, well, her companion of the previous evening... and the previous night... *all* of the previous night – pass without a rejoinder. Harold watched her closely and could tell exactly what was going on in her mind as she sought the appropriate words for a stinging rebuttal. He was about to say something when Ruby, who had squared her shoulders in preparation for launching a tirade of her own verbal abuse at the innocent woman, slumped back in her chair and slowly turned to look at him. He could tell from her expression that the light had dawned.

"She means that as a compliment, doesn't she?" she stated more than asked. Her voice was low, subdued.

"I believe so, yes," Harold acknowledged, taking his turn to try to look demure. He did not succeed nearly as well as she had a few moments earlier. "The *true* Desert Rats, though, depending on whose version you prefer to accept, were either our own Seventh Armoured Division or the Ninth Australian Division who held out for so long and so valiantly at Tobruk. Personally, I think the Aussies are the most deserving of the name. Rommel put it about that he had them bottled up 'like rats in a trap' you see and..."

"You were in North Africa before...?"

"Yes," he nodded. "And nowadays just about anyone who was there..."

"How *long*? I mean, how long have you been at it?" she searched his face for clues.

"That depends on what you mean by 'it'," he shrugged. "I joined the Territorials in April of '39," he explained matter-of-factly. "I was called up in August. Spent what seemed like, at the time, half a lifetime in training... including a two-year holiday in Scotland," he added circumspectly. "But I didn't cross the water, as they say, until late November '42. Muddled about in Algeria and Tunisia for a few months until they shipped us over here last October."

As her eyes darted back and forth from one to the other of Harold's, Ruby's face screwed up into an expression that held both concern and incredulity. His own gaze mirrored the concern, but the incredulity was replaced with confusion. Finally, closing her eyes, she let out a deep sigh.

"My God, how do you do it?" she almost seemed to beg. "I've been here scarcely more than a month and I'm already finding it a tremendous strain just trying to hold myself together at times. You've been in this nightmare from the beginning and yet you still manage to smile and laugh." She opened her eyes and looked directly at him again. "You... you're so controlled, so calm, so confident and self-assured! I..."

"It's not as though I – we – have a lot of options," he broke in. "But don't kid yourself, my sweet young innocent. I'm none of those things you just attributed to me."

"O, but you *are*. You..."

"I'm scared silly most of the time," he interrupted again. "My hands shake so much when I shave myself that I cut myself almost every morning. I've taken to letting Nobby do it, as he seems to enjoy pampering me."

"Nobby?" she queried raising an eyebrow.

"My batman," Harold explained. "Couldn't survive without him. Now *there's* a man deserving of your praise. *His* hands don't shake at all," he asserted.

"Yes, but you..." Ruby tried to pick up where she had left off.

"I do what I have to do because there is no other choice. That's true for all of us here. It's no different for you or for the other sisters or the doctors or the Generals or the Privates. You do your best to keep going and to stay alive and to stay sane."

He leaned across the table and took both of Ruby's hands in his. "And you seize every possible ounce of joy, every fleeting moment of pleasure, every bit of human warmth and companionship that you can because... because..."

"Because it may be your last!" Ruby finished for him. He squeezed her hands then raised them to his lips and kissed them one finger at a time.

"'Atta boy, Mister Rat!" came the hearty encouragement of the corpulent English nurse at the next table as she rose and carried away her empty tray. "Looks to me it'll soon be Mister and *Missus* Rat, 'less I miss my guess," she chortled loudly as she waddled away.

IN THE DRAWING ROOM
March 31, 1944

"Do you suppose it's one of those lovely sandy beaches that would have attracted family picnics and scantily clad young women before the war?" Walter ruminated.

"Afraid I couldn't say," answered Cecil. "I suppose Italy has its own Riviera region or Gold Coast... strikes me that just about *every* country on the Mediterranean claims to have those. But whether or not this 'Anzio Beach' is located in such an area I have no idea. Why do you ask?"

"Well, I was just thinking," said Walter. "As long as the poor Americans are stuck there it might be nice for them if they were laying in soft warm sand rather than a bed of rocks and pebbles."

"Devilishly difficult to pitch a tent in soft sand, you know!" Cecil quipped. "Still, I suspect they have a good deal more important things to worry about than that."

16

BARI, ITALY
April 1944

"Doin' the Lambeth Walk!" shouted the young Lieutenant, raising his beer glass to the approving chorus of dozens of others in the ballroom of the old hotel. It was the third or fourth time that they had called for that particular piece that evening. Harold complied. He was so happy he would have played a German marching song if someone had asked for it. Many of the officers and nursing sisters sang along, most as boisterously as the old tune demanded and most out of tune but no one really cared. They were miles from the front and their spirits were high. They were *alive!*

In many ways it was a scene that had been replayed half a dozen times since Captain Lawes and "that little Canuck beauty" had become an item three short weeks ago. Tonight, however, was different. At least it certainly felt different.

That afternoon Ruby had agreed to marry him. Catherine and Nobby had been made privy to the happy news but no one else knew.

The attendant celebrants were all tired. Tired beyond any state of fatigue they might have conceived of before this experience of war. They were all afraid. Even more afraid than when as infants they had imagined the bogeyman to be real. And they were resigned to the fact that Fate had put them in this place at this time. But most of all they were desperate. Desperate for *anything* that would relieve them, if only for a short while, of their fatigue, their fear, their resignation. And while the bountiful alcohol, the unlimited supply of American cigarettes, the unaffected companionship, and the joining of voices in song all helped, mostly it was Captain Lawes and his piano playing.

The secretly betrothed couple had walked directly across the room to a table beside the piano around which several staff officers were seated with the Matron and a few nursing sisters. They were warmly greeted, and room was made for Ruby to sit at the table while Harold turned toward the piano. He approached the gray-haired Colonel Mitchell who for the past half-hour had been doing a quite respectable job of picking out the melodies with his right hand only of some of the more popular tunes, so that those in the room so inclined could sing along.

The colonel, Chief of Surgery at Ruby's Base Hospital – First Canadian General – looked up and the frown of concentration that had sculpted his face a moment before melted into a broad and heartfelt smile. He jumped up from the piano bench, nearly tipping it over in the process, grasped Harold by the elbow, and guided him to the keyboard. Harold sat down at the piano, the Colonel patting him vigorously on the back and smiling all the while. As the Colonel returned to the table planting a fatherly kiss on Ruby's cheek, Harold glanced over to her, one eyebrow raised. She smiled at him and mouthed "Whispering!"

His hands glided over the keyboard so smoothly and rapidly it seemed as if he wasn't even touching the keys and yet somehow the beautiful, delicate melody of his signature tune was being produced. It was *so* beautiful that for almost a full minute everyone in the crowded, smoke-filled room stopped talking and just listened.

Someone started to applaud. Someone else cheered. The enchanted moment ended as abruptly as it had begun, conversation returning almost to normal levels but not quite. The singers took up their inharmonious chorus again. Two officers rose from the table where Ruby was seated and invited two of the nursing sisters to dance. Within seconds the tiny dance floor was crowded with impromptu couples. Harold was at the piano the whole time, his marvelous playing seemingly effortless and his repertoire seemingly inexhaustible.

"Nothing like personally providing the entertainment at your own party," he thought. But of course, no one else present save Catherine realized that "Mr. and Mrs. Rat," as they had become widely known were now actually

engaged to be married. This was an engagement party that only four people in the world knew about. And Nobby was fast asleep in the back of a lorry four miles away.

His playing was constant, uninterrupted. There were no breaks between tunes. Someone would shout out the name of another song even as the last notes of the current piece were fading from the throats of those around. And he would somehow fashion a transition from whatever he was currently playing into the desired piece, changes of key or tempo presenting no obstacle. Even when he lit a cigarette or took a drink – various members of his appreciative audience kept lining up shot glasses brimming with Triple Sec on top of the piano – he kept his left hand going, flowing over the keys.

Almost seven hours had elapsed when he finally stood up from the piano bench… and promptly sat back down. He looked up at the shot glasses on the piano and tried to count them, but it was beyond him. Then she was at his side helping him to stand, steadying him as they made their way toward the exit.

She helped him to climb in behind the wheel of the lorry he had commandeered for the evening, ran around, and climbed in beside him. He started the engine, depressed the clutch, and put it in gear. They moved off smoothly. Even in his obviously intoxicated condition, driving was almost second nature to him. In an unfamiliar city under blackout conditions, however, seeing where he was going was another matter entirely.

"Are you sure you know where you're going, Mr. Rat?" she asked. "It's pitch black out there!"

It was three or four o'clock in the morning. A cool, dense fog clung to their clothes, their skin, and the windscreen, obscuring the view and restricting vision to perhaps ten feet. No moon or stars showed to provide even a hint of light. There were no streetlamps, there was no light spilling from the windows of the nearby buildings, no other vehicles on the road. And the headlights of the vehicle they were in were not, by design and by order, illuminated.

"Not to worry, Mrs. Rat," he replied although it sounded more like "nawdhoowurrhy mizzizzraght." He took a drag on his cigarette and turned to smile at her. "'f we go too farrh *oouest* we shtar' goin' *up!* 'f we go too farrh *easht* we shtar' goin' *dowwwn!*" He shifted up through the gears and accelerated. "'shlong as we stay on lev'l groun'," he turned to smile at her again, "we *cann-nott*' possibly go wrong! *Truss* me!"

At that point the three-tonne lorry shot out over the end of the dock and into the Adriatic Sea.

Catherine saved the day.

When 'Mrs. Rat' didn't show up for her 5:00 a.m. rounds at the base hospital that morning, Catherine went looking for her. She knew where to look. She didn't find her friend nor her friend's English Captain, but she did find Nobby and sent him off immediately to search for them.

He found them only ten minutes later. They were sharing the last cigarette they possessed between them, still sitting in the lorry, which was firmly stuck in the muck just a few feet from the end of the dock. The water only came up to the axles. Within the hour he had arranged with one of the Company's NCOs to have them towed out.

By now 'Mr. Rat' was more or less sober but a severe headache made him wince every time he moved. The lorry was not damaged – well, not badly – and he wasn't scheduled for duty until 0800 hours, so he wasn't too worried for himself.

'Mrs. Rat' on the other hand was going to catch hell and it was *his* fault. She was being awfully good about it which only made him feel worse.

They were married as covertly as possible in Naples on April 4, 1944.

Officially any woman in the Canadian Red Cross Corps who got married was to be sent back to London immediately, but Ruby was having none of that. That's why she had insisted, over Harold's protestations, that their marriage be kept quiet. She knew she was needed here and was determined to continue making her contribution. Besides, she wanted to stay close to her new husband. Harold tried again and again to persuade her otherwise, but it was no use.

Harold had surprised himself by getting over Betty's faithlessness and the divorce far more readily and more quickly than he would have believed possible. At first he put it down to the constant pressures of his command, assuming that the unceasing and ineluctable workload served as a narcotic, anesthetizing his emotions or at least distracting him sufficiently so he had no time to dwell on them. But gradually he came to understand that the only real hurt was to his pride, his self-esteem. And once he realized that he had to admit to himself that he had never really loved Betty after all. He had reached this conclusion only a few days before that fateful evening when he had been told by Catherine none too politely in the beginning to, "Stop playing that damned piano this instant, you heartless beast!"

Now he had fallen in love—only this time he knew it was for real. "All is known in comparison," as the old proverb says and compared to what he had thought was love for Betty there could be no doubt at all what he was feeling for Ruby. What's more, she obviously felt the same way about him.

For a short time, it looked as though there would be no opportunity for the romance to blossom. The day after their Naming-Day breakfast Harold had been ordered to move his Company to San Severo about 150 miles away from Barletta and was kept extremely busy for the next two days. Then the malaria returned with a vengeance and he was ordered to bed with instructions to "avoid sleeping in wet blankets beneath lorries." He was slow to recover, eventually being given leave and sent back to the 8th Army Rest Camp at Bari.

Ruby found him there just as the light of day was dawning. Like several others in the smoke-filled room he was sitting in a big, overstuffed easy chair, reading, with the trademark cigarette-dangling-from-the-corner-of-the-lower-lip.

She crossed her right foot over her left and leaned against the doorjamb. "Well, well! Hello there, Mister Rat!" she sang out. "Fancy meeting *you* here!" Every head in the room snapped up smartly, eyes riveted on the shapely figure backlit in the doorway by the rising sun. None of them could see her face or more precisely, her eyes, so no one at first could determine which of them she was looking at. To whom had she spoken? Seconds ticked by.

"I suppose you've come all this way for a song," Harold replied pretending to return to his reading. A few heads, the disappointment obvious in their eyes or in their body posture did just that. But most held their gaze, whether out of curiosity or simply because they liked what they were looking at. "Very well then, *Missus Rat*. You shall have it!" Abandoning any further pretense Harold sprang out of the chair, crossed the intervening space between them in three great strides, and swept her into his arms.

Ruby's presence at the Rest Camp was like a tonic for Harold. Within three days of her arrival he was back to normal.

Over the next few days, they managed to see a great deal of one another—more than either could have reasonably hoped for under the circumstances. On more than one occasion when they were separated by only a short distance geographically – anything less than 50 miles – Harold would go out of camp on his motorcycle, ostensibly to reconnoiter but in fact to effect a clandestine rendezvous with his sweetheart. Singing along *en français* to his own accompaniment on a piano or when he could find one an accordion, he courted her with "*J'Attendrai*," "*Seul Ce Soir*," and a few compositions of his own.

The next time they made love it was under the moon and stars of the Italian sky in a roofless bombed-out farmhouse. They were not far from the Canadian Fourth Casualty Clearing Station where Ruby had been assigned and where he had collected her only three and a half hours after the end of her seemingly endless shift. Afterwards they were sitting in bed, naked, smoking cigarettes and drinking scotch when some would-be thieves attempted to force their way in through the only door. At first terrified, Ruby was soon beside herself with laughter, hugging a pillow to her stomach because she was laughing so hard that it hurt her tender ribs.

Harold had jumped off the bed, snatched up his pistol, and emptied it through the flimsy door. From outside came a series of screams and curses followed immediately by thumping and scuffling noises as the would-be robbers beat a hasty retreat. But not before Harold, still stark naked, had slipped a new clip into his pistol, flung open the door, and fired five more shots—into the air, as the bandits were clearly no longer interested in their erstwhile objective.

Late in March, when Harold was back in Barletta for a couple of days, Ruby invited him to Canadian-hosted party at the First Canadian General Hospital. It was cluster of old school buildings that had somehow managed to remain more or less intact. It was intended to be an affair for senior officers only but since Harold's piano playing was well known and well liked, Ruby had easily wangled an invitation for him.

The party was held in what had been the school's auditorium. All the brass were there, including Harold's CO, now Lieutenant Colonel Stoville. Two hours into the evening, alcohol in all its potable forms – beer, wine, liquor, liqueurs – had been flowing freely. Colonel Stoville was known to have developed a taste for Canadian rye whiskey and had just finished loudly complimenting his hosts on the quality of the Seagram's they were serving.

Ruby leaned over Harold's shoulder as he was playing the piano and whispered, "Watch this!" She promptly left the room.

The senior Canadian doctor, Colonel Mitchell or simply "Mitch" to his associates, smiled at Colonel Stoville in acknowledgment of his outspoken appreciation of the Seagram's.

"You are obviously a gentleman of discerning tastes," he flattered Stoville, loudly enough to attract the attention of everyone within 20 feet. "As you have been so generous in your praise of our humble everyday whiskey, perhaps I could entice you to sample some of my Special Reserve."

The intrigued onlookers fell silent and gathered around the two men.

At this point Ruby came back into the room weaving through the crowd and carrying a silver tray on one hand high above her head like an accomplished waitress. She set the tray on the piano. It contained two crystal old-fashioned glasses and a dark brown bottle with no label. Mitch strolled over to the tray, poured two fingers of colourless liquid into each glass, and motioned for Colonel Stoville to join him.

"It's an acquired taste, as you Brit's like to say of your scotch whiskey," he explained seriously to Stoville. "But I'm sure *you* will appreciate it, Colonel." He sipped from his own glass, making a show of rolling the liquor around on his tongue and inhaling deeply before swallowing.

"Ahh," he sighed, closing his eyes. "Pure ambrosia!"

Harold's friend and CO eagerly took up his glass, a grin like that of a mischievous child on his face, and raised it to his lips. Mimicking his host, he slowly and ostentatiously savoured his first sip. "By God, that's smooth!" he proclaimed and took a heartier swallow. "But it's nothing like rye whiskey. What is it?" he demanded, emptying his glass and reaching for the bottle to refill it.

"We here at the hospital call it Mitch's Milk," the doctor answered, pouring half a teaspoon's worth of the liquor from his own glass onto the floor. He set his glass on the tray, removed a book of matches from his pocket, and squatted down beside the tiny viscous pool of liquid. "A little something I whipped up in the lab a few weeks ago when our usual ration of rye was delayed," he continued, striking a match and setting it to the liquor.

An orange flame almost three feet high erupted for a moment then settled back leaving a small constant blue-green flame only two inches tall.

Those gathered around stared at the flame waiting for it to go out, for the fuel to be exhausted. But it just kept burning and burning and as each minute passed Colonel Stoville's face turned greener and greener!

They laughed whenever they could. They looked for excuses to laugh, however unlikely, however bizarre. It was pure escapism and they knew it, but dear God how they *needed* it.

IN THE DRAWING ROOM
April 14, 1944

"I'm not so sure it's a good thing, Cecil, not at all." Walter was clearly struggling with his emotions.

"Listen my friend. Where's the harm in it?" asked Cecil, trying to be helpful. "Don't try to pretend you're going senile on me and can't remember what it was like to be young and in love!"

"Of *course* I remember," spluttered a downcast Walter. "That's what's worrying me."

"Oh, for the sake of..." Cecil inhaled deeply trying to gather his arguments.

"And you remember too!" Walter accused loudly. This gave Cecil pause. "All right, perhaps neither one of us was 'repulsive' to look at but you have to admit, Cecil, we were no Valentinos either. It was the *uniform* that did it I tell you... the uniform and... and the times."

Cecil exhaled and it suddenly dawned on him that he had been holding his breath all through Walter's diatribe.

"That may be, Walter," he soothed. "But are you really trying to convince me that you regret having married your Annie?"

"No, no, no! It's not that at all!" Walter protested. "Anyway... that was different."

"Oh, come now!" Cecil taunted. "A dashing young midshipman in full dress uniform with his picture gracing the front pages of every newspaper in the country meets a young lady at a commemorative ball held in his honour and sweeps her off her feet. Is it so different?"

"Well..." the big man grumbled, covering his face with both hands, "...it's just that..."

"So, Major Buchkowski only got his picture on the third page of *The Stars and Stripes*. It wasn't a commemorative ball held in his honour, only an ENSA show that he just happened to be attending. But then your Annie *just happened* to have been invited to the festivities at which you were being honoured. As your niece *just happened* to be on volunteer duty at the ENSA club that night. Allowing for these minor discrepancies, the fact remains, my friend, that he too is a decorated war hero. And while I am no expert on the matter, I would venture to say that your niece Julia is every bit as much in love with him today as Annie was with you 30 years ago."

"It's *different*, I tell you," Walter stubbornly persisted. He had been mustering his own arguments for several days now. "To begin with by today's standards morality is lax to put it politely!"

"Ah now we come to it at last." Cecil had anticipated this line of thought. "You needn't blush on my account, Walter. For at least a year after Annie succumbed to the cancer you made a conceit of the fact that the two of you were virgins on your wedding night."

Walter turned three shades of red.

"And every time you boasted of that... what would I do in response... *hmn?*"

Walter could tell from the expression on Cecil's face or from the shared experiences of their long acquaintance that his friend did not mean to be cruel.

"You, uhm..." clearing his throat, "... you would recount in graphic detail one of your seemingly innumerable conquests."

Walter raised a clenched fist in Cecil's direction and shook it three times to punctuate: "While – (*pump!*) – in (*pump!*) – uniform! (*big pump!*)"

"And was your regard for me... your... *respect* for me as your friend... Was it in any way poisoned or diluted by my recounting to you those anecdotal frivolities of my youth?" Cecil asked.

Rather than answer a direct question Walter clung to the last hope in his distorted assessment of the circumstances.

"At least Annie was..." Walter hesitated. Cecil had known that Walter would not surrender gracefully and shuddered to think what his close friend of so many years might be about to say what he feared.

"What I mean is, for Annie and me the whole thing transpired here, at home, on English soil. Annie's roots go back almost as far as my own to Saxon times! This... this twice times foreigner, this Major Buchkowsy, a... a Polish-American..."

"Shut up!" Cecil commanded. "Shut up, *now!*" Incensed, he abruptly stood up, glaring down at his rotund friend as he imagined Zeus might have glared down from Mount Olympus as he was preparing to hurl a lightning bolt. "If they're good enough to fight for us, side by side with our boys... good enough to *die* for us, side by side with our boys...

"There are *already* American *bastards*..." Walter whimpered.

"Shame on you, Sir! Shame, I say!" Cecil thundered, attracting altogether too much attention from others in the drawing room.

Registering the attentive, inquisitive glances of those gathered Cecil lowered his voice. "Have you so little trust, Walter, in your niece's virtue? Have you so little faith... in the power of love?"

Mr.& Mrs. Rat, Avellino, June 1944

Officers' Mess, Mandolfo, September 1944

17

CASSINO, ITALY
May 1944

March had been witness to the third major assault on Monte Cassino, this time spearheaded by the New Zealanders. It was no more successful than the earlier attempts. Just after 2300 hours on May 11th General Alexander threw everything the combined forces of the Eighth Army had at its disposal against the stubbornly recalcitrant remnants of the Germans' Gustav Line.

In the Canadian 4th CCS, Ruby and her fellow nurses assisted Colonel Mitchell and other doctors in the operating theatres. With artillery bursting around them casualties were brought in so quickly and in such numbers that they could not possibly cope. Every 20 minutes or so a large canvas laundry hamper was wheeled into the operating room as another was wheeled out, filled to capacity with arms, legs, hands, and feet that had had to be amputated.

Despite her training and her resolve Ruby vomited up everything she tried to eat or drink for three days running before she finally forced herself under control. As if to prove to herself that she really *did* have control she devised a sort of test for herself. She would hold both arms straight out in front of her palms down and have Catherine place two brimming glasses of water on them. She would stand like that for a count of 100 without spilling a drop while the carnage and destruction swirled about her.

A few days earlier Harold had been ordered to provide transport for a small contingent of Gurkhas to the base of a hill on The Gustav Line just a little northeast of Monte Cassino. Harold had never before actually been exposed to the renowned Gurkhas, but he knew that they were reputed to be possibly the best, most loyal and most fearless fighters among all of His Majesty's assorted military forces.

Harold drove the lead vehicle. They took only four lorries, although three would have sufficed to carry the 39 men, and they started out around midnight. The objective was to kidnap one or two of the enemy and bring them back to camp for questioning in the hope of gaining some intelligence concerning the defenses and the disposition of the forces arrayed against the allies. At the appointed destination, the Gurkhas disembarked and silently disappeared into the night.

Harold and his drivers waited, half a dozen Ghurkas remaining with them as guards. It seemed a long wait but in fact it was scarcely more than two hours before the Nepalese corporal who was in charge of the six-man guard unit motioned for Harold to start his engine. Doing so he could just make out in the blackness of night the returning soldiers. As they streamed past him he heard some incomprehensible thumping noises in the back of the lorry. Finally, gagged and bound, the German prisoner was dragged by. Harold felt and heard the wretched man's struggles as he was hauled into the back of the truck and secured. Then the Gurkha corporal was beside him calmly signalling that it was time to go.

Delighted and at the same time somewhat disappointed that the evening's adventure had come off without incident, Harold and his three drivers pulled into camp shortly before dawn. The very, very English Officer Commanding of the Gurkha unit was there to meet them. He stepped up to the front bumper of Harold's lorry as he and the Gurkha Corporal climbed out.

"Good hunting this night, Corporal?" he asked, ignoring Harold.

"Very good hunting this night, Sir!" the corporal responded flashing a broad smile of gleaming white teeth that stood out in his dark face even in the scant pre-dawn light. He saluted and gestured toward the rear of the lorry. The officer nodded and they started off. Harold, virtually forgotten, followed.

"One live prisoner as ordered, Sir!" beamed the corporal, throwing back the tarpaulin and lowering the tailgate. All was darkness in the confines of the truck.

"Show a light!" commanded the officer.

Two nearby Gurkhas hurried to obey, pulling powerful flashlights from their webbing. The beams converged on the prisoner's face. He was gagged and tied, standing, his arms pulled out like a crucifixion by taught ropes stretching to the top rungs of the superstructure that supported the canvas covering the bed of the lorry. His eyes were completely vacant.

"What's this then?" demanded the officer, snatching one of the flashlights and playing its beam around the bed of the truck. Harold took one look, turned away, and was violently ill.

Incredible soldiers that they were, the small Gurkha unit had stealthily penetrated behind enemy sentries, silently killing more than a dozen as they progressed. They had then come upon a full Company of German soldiers sleeping the sleep of utter exhaustion. Having first made certain of their assignment by subduing a dozing *Oberleutnant,* they had then proceeded methodically with their infamous viciously curved *kukri* knives to cut off the heads of every sleeping enemy soldier they could find.

Harold was told later that there were 76 heads in the back of the lorry. The lone live prisoner, who had spent the journey back to camp tied up in that lorry, had understandably gone stark raving mad and was incapable of providing any useful information.

Hell was being redefined. They were caught in the embrace of a nightmare so vast and so horrific that it was mind numbing. Feelings and emotions ran the gamut from strained to tortured, from raw to rancid. The worst part of it all was that they were not alone. Tens of thousands of fellow human beings on both sides were being subjected to the same stupefying terrors, the same paralyzing fears, the same morbid despair. And there was no respite in sight. Each new day brought appalling revelations, hideous experiences, grisly, sometimes ghoulish sights beyond anything that the sickest imagination could have conceived before... before this *reality.* And each virtually sleepless night was filled with a profound dread and the oh so tenuous battle with one's *Self* to find the necessary courage to continue.

Mostly Harold and Ruby drew upon one another for strength. As well, with no hesitation or remorse, they drew upon the strengths of their many mutual friends and acquaintances, as and when appropriate—appropriate in the sense that it was necessary for both of them, but it also worked the other way. Their friends seemed to have greater need of them more frequently than vice versa. And they seemed to have more to give. They looked for any excuse to laugh. Any excuse.

IN THE DRAWING ROOM
May 23, 1944

"Trench foot! Are you sure? God, I thought we had done with that once and for all, you know, back in '18." Bitter personal memories echoed in Cecil's strained speech.

"'...including, but not limited to, chilblains, dysentery, malaria, toxemia, trench foot, typhus, and scabies,'" Walter quoted sonorously from the newspaper article. "'It is estimated that at least one man in three, (and some authorities suggest that this is a conservative view) is partially or totally debilitated by disease or infection.'" He concluded.

"But... what about that new wonder drug, um... penicillium, er... penicillin?" Cecil groused.

"In the first place, Cecil," Walter adopted a lecturing pose, "even penicillin does not cure *every* malady known to afflict modern man. In the second place – and more to the point – they simply can't produce enough of the stuff fast enough to keep up with demand."

"Not even the Americans?" griped Cecil. "Roosevelt boasted they were 'the arsenal of democracy.'"

"Ah, yes, well..." Walter demurred, "I believe it was tanks and battleships that he had in mind at the time."

18

ITALY'S ADRIATIC COAST
May through August 1944

On May 3rd Harold had been posted to 78 Bulk Petroleum Company in Vasto north of Termoli. After, Cassino had finally fallen. II Polish Corps had raised a hastily improvised flag over the ruins of the monastery on May 18th following five months of horrifying carnage. Kesselring had grudgingly pulled the German 10th Army back from The Gustav Line. Now 78 Company along with the bulk of the British 8th Army bolstered by strong Polish and Canadian contingents gradually forced their way up Italy's Adriatic coast and through the rugged hills of Umbria in the centre.

Toward the end of May American forces under Clark finally broke out of their beach head at Anzio. On June 4th they entered Rome. On June 6th the Allies launched the invasion of Normandy and those in Italy became 'the forgotten army.' The tune of "Lilli Marlene" now served as the backdrop for the 8th Army's new campaign song.

> *We are the D-Day Dodgers, out in Italy*
> *Always on the vino, always on the spree.*
> *Eighth Army skivers and their tanks,*
> *We go to war in ties like swanks.*
> *For we're the D-Day Dodgers, in sunny Italy.*

We landed at Salerno, a holiday with pay.
Jerry brought his bands out to cheer us on the way,
Showed us the sights and gave us tea,
We all sang songs, the beer was free
For we are the D-Day Dodgers, the lads that D-Day dodged.

Palermo and Cassino were taken in our stride,
We did not go to fight there, we just went for the ride.
Anzio and Sangro are just names,
We only went to look for dames,
For we are the D-Day Dodgers, in sunny Italy

Look around the hillsides, through the mist and rain,
See the scattered crosses, some that bear no name.
Blood, tears, sweat and toil are gone,
The lads beneath, they slumber on.
These are your D-Day Dodgers, who'll stay in Italy.

Over the coming weeks and months as the relentless struggles continued many more verses would be added.

For almost two weeks after the liberation of Rome the Allied armies had every reason to hope that they had at last broken the spirit of their foe. Kesselring's forces looked to be in full retreat, demolishing roads and bridges as they went and laying minefields behind them but fighting only a cautious rearguard action. It took only 12 days for the Fifth Army, comprised of American and British troops under Clark, to advance another 90 miles to the north of Rome. But then the going got tougher. Over the next three weeks they managed only 45 miles with casualties mounting steadily.

Kesselring had been using the precious time to reinforce his strongest line of defense yet: The Gothic Line. Zigzagging 200 miles across the breadth of northern Italy, The Gothic line formed a ten-mile deep obstacle belt consisting of minefields, barbed wire barriers, and anti-tank ditches. There were 30 tank turrets with the now infamous 88 mm guns mounted on bases of concrete and steel, 2,376 machine-gun nests, 479 artillery positions, and miles of trenches and steel-reinforced redoubts to shelter the infantry. Troops and supplies moved swiftly along the main highway connecting Rimini, Bologna, and Milan, which ran just behind the defensive line. The crafty old German General understood – and knew that the advancing Allied Generals also understood – if he could hold the defensive line until the onset of winter, he would have gained invaluable breathing space.

The race was on. The pace was measured. In the west the Fifth Army liberated Perugia, Ancona, Siena, and Livorno and reached the Arno river by early August. Before the month was out, they added Florence to their list of conquests. Although the truth of the matter was that Kesselring had forbidden any fighting in that beautiful historic city and had quietly withdrawn his troops after blowing up or blockading any bridges that might have facilitated the Allies' pursuit

Meanwhile to the east, another wily old General by the name of Alexander, commanding the Eighth Army, had a trump card or two of his own to play.

On August 25th he surprised the Germans with an attack well north of the position he had been ostensibly content just to hold on the Adriatic coast. As he had hoped the Germans fell back to regroup and as they were doing so he sent troops across the Metauro river south of Pesaro. The Service Corps quickly bridged the waterway so that others might follow. The Germans in this sector prudently withdrew to the formidable defenses of The Gothic Line.

Some pundits would argue after the event that given Lieutenant General Mark Clark's established track record of notable disregard for the orders of High Command (in favour of pursuing any path that might enhance his personal reputation), it was once more only the desire for more self-glorification that had prompted him to push across the Arno river and to capture Pisa on September 2nd. Ergo, they argued, it was pure serendipity that the Germans were deceived into believing that this was to be the focal point of the main attack while Alexander's August 25th attack on the east coast had been a mere feint and accordingly rushed reinforcements to the west.

Those same self-appointed experts would subsequently learn that for more than two weeks prior to his August 25th feint, Alexander had been quietly moving eight entire divisions of the Eighth Army with support corps and tens of thousands of vehicles from central Italy over the Apennines to the coast. On September 12th with his opposition fortuitously diminished he launched his main offensive.

Over a 30-mile front Alexander's courageous soldiers attacked. Within hours they had breached the ineffable Gothic Line and captured the key position of San Fortunato. Before nightfall they entered Rimini—the tail-end of The Gothic Line itself.

"Ortona in June; Guilianova in July; Falconara by late August." War diary entries were supposed to be made daily, but Harold had fallen behind. He shuffled the bits and pieces of paper in front of him – hastily scribbled notes to himself for his journal that had accumulated over the past weeks – studiously attempting to put them in some order. The rickety table trembled slightly beneath his hands, and the earth groaned in protest to the current artillery barrage. The shadows cast by the light from the kerosene lamp flickered on the side of the tent. He sipped at the lukewarm tea that Nobby had brought him 15 minutes ago. The handwriting in front of him slowly went out of focus.

Reflecting on his Commando days and particularly on the bitter-sweet memories of that day when Colonel Simmons had come to inform him of his reassignment to the RASC, he couldn't help but wonder at all that had transpired since and whether indeed there was not some Higher Power watching over him and guiding his life. For half a year now the violent deaths and indescribable sufferings of so many of those around him had become his constant companions. True he had seen both death and grievous injury with the Commandos, but there had always been at least a brief reprieve, a healing time, between missions. No such luxury offered itself in his present circumstances. And the Commandos had never had to contend for more than a day or two with the more insidious afflictions that tormented the poor valiant bastards with whom he had toiled in North Africa and was now sweating with in Italy. Unceasing enemy fire, day after day, night after night; disease so rampant and varied and wide spread as to defy all the Florence Nightingales ever born; the elements that on any given day, invariably, perversely, seemed to favour the enemy; short rations and shorter tempers.

Why then was *he* still relatively whole? What quirk of Fortune's grace… what whim of that elusive Higher Power had so far delivered him from the common fate of so many others around him? Might it truly be Divine Intervention that brought Ruby into his life?

Ruby and the No. 1 Canadian General Hospital remained in Avellino. Over three months she and Harold managed to see one another only twice, when Harold came down to Naples on an errand for a few days in late May and again at the end of June.

Then on August 24th No. 1 CGH was moved up to Iesi, or Jesi as most called it, just a few miles inland from Falconara. The nursing sisters and welfare officers travelled in the backs of trucks that lumbered and bumped their way along the pitted, broken roads at what seemed barely more than a good walking pace. It was a hot and, for once, dry day. The dust churned up by the trucks hung in the air and caked on perspiring faces. Everyone in the trucks was soon covered in it but the Italian civilians, riding in donkey carts or trudging along the roadside on foot, were even worse off. Ragged, dirty, and hungry they were a pitiful sight.

"They say mud packs are good for the skin," Ruby told Catherine loudly, trying to lighten the sombre mood that settled over the group as they watched the lines of doleful Italians. "Do you suppose that *dust* packs are any good?"

Her clumsy effort at humour did not even elicit a chuckle, only a few wry grins. But it did break the mood for a short while and the others in the back of the truck struck up conversations again, doing their best not to think about the tragic lives of the dispossessed who were walking alongside the convoy. But at their lunch stop in a field that had been cleared of mines only that morning, the civilians gathered around them like vultures at a carcass, poised to jump upon any least morsel of food that might be cast off.

The Canadians queued up to collect their sandwiches from the back of the mess truck then moved into the roped-off area of the field designated safe from buried mines and sat in circles on the grass.

One of the nursing sisters stood up again almost immediately, mumbling that she wasn't really hungry. She walked cautiously toward a woman at the edge of the field who was carrying an infant and had a toddler clinging to her skirts. The sister reached out to give the young mother her sandwich. The woman snatched food from the sister's hand and started to turn away, but before she had even turned around three or four other hands reached out and ripped the bread and its contents into bits. Half a dozen people fell to their knees, scrabbling in the dust with fingers and even their mouths like ravenous dogs falling upon their prey. Fighting broke out and one of the officers had to rush over and fire his revolver into the air several times before a semblance of order could be restored.

The well-meaning nursing sister returned to the circle of seated co-workers, slowly sank to her knees, put her face in her hands, and cried. Ruby moved to her side.

"It makes your heart ache, I know," she said to the sob-racked woman. "To think of us sitting here eating while these poor people stand around just... watching. The food sticks in your throat. But you *must* eat," she continued, knowing that all the others in the circle were listening, too.

"Look, our food is rationed to the bare necessities as it is, and you must keep your strength up. You don't need to be reminded how important our work here is or how much we all depend on you to do your part. Our boys depend on you, too."

This only caused the distraught young woman to sob louder.

"Look at me!" Ruby commanded roughly.

The sister lifted her tear-stained face from her hands and looked at Ruby.

"Listen, love!" Ruby went on, putting a comforting hand on the woman's cheek. "There is nothing we can do for them right now. If we all gave all our sandwiches to them it still wouldn't be enough. And if we gave them our dinner rations tonight it still wouldn't be enough. And tomorrow *we* would all be weaker from hunger and next-to-useless when the first convoy of ambulances carrying *our* wounded boys pulls into the hospital we're going to set up tonight! If we have the energy," she stressed, fixing the other woman's eyes with her own.

"Here, love. Eat!" she ended, forcing half of her own sandwich into the sister's trembling hands.

Harold was ecstatic when he learned of the Canadian hospital's move up to Iesi. The afternoon following their arrival, though he could only get away for a couple of hours, he borrowed the OC's Humber and drove over to Iesi in the hope of finding his beloved bride. He did.

That's when she told him that she thought she was pregnant.

IN THE DRAWING ROOM
June 30, 1944

"I do not for the life of me understand why people insist on calling the bloody things 'doodlebugs'! Makes them sound cute when in fact they are deadly!" Walter proclaimed. "And just when it was beginning to look as though we had the blighters on the run and the end was near!"

"I don't know which is worse..." Cecil agreed, "...the actual explosion or that interminable blood curdling silence after the engine cuts out and there's nothing you can do but wait... wait for the potential violent ending of your life."

He closed his eyes and buried his face in his hands. "Or worse still... the guilt and the shame. The terrible guilt and shame of the unavoidable sense of relief one feels when the cursed thing finally detonates killing somebody else and leaving you breathing."

"That was true in the trenches, Cecil, or on the deck of a ship. If a bullet was meant for someone else, well..." Walter rationalized.

"But these are innocent civilians we're talking about, damn it!" Cecil shouted. "They can't even vent their anger or mitigate their fear by shooting back!"

"From all that we've learned about the diabolical minds of the Nazis to date," Walter expounded eruditely, "I should say these new weapons are designed expressly with that in mind. They are meant not so much to inflict damage as they are to instill fear and engender terror."

Cecil held his friend's sympathetic gaze.

"Unfortunately, Walter, if I'm any example the damnable things are succeeding."

19

BETWEEN RAVENNA & ANCONA, ITALY
September through October 1944

The hospital at Iesi consisted of a few large tents, which served as admitting and discharge rooms, the operating theatre, and the mess, surrounded by the smaller two-person tents that provided the living quarters for the staff and at one end the inevitable three-sided bivvy.

All of this was pitched high up on the side of a mountain. The little tents were regularly blown away in the gusty winds or washed away in the torrential downpour. There were fleas that got into your bedding and bit you; mosquitoes that got under your netting and stung you; spiders and beetles that dropped into your hair and terrified you; wasps that got into your jam before you could spread it; and lizards that crept into your rubber boots and startled you when you slipped your feet into them in the mornings.

Rations were short and unappetizing, a typical dinner menu comprised of boiled white beans and bully beef or anemic soy sausages and lumpy gray mashed potatoes. It was a veritable treat when occasionally one of the girls managed to buy or to trade for a couple of black-market eggs. And it was truly astonishing to witness the creativity that blossomed trying to figure out how best to apportion those two little eggs among at least six people.

Ruby and Catherine were happily partnered in one of the little tents. Each evening they were provided with a canvas bucket of water. By morning it was crusted with ice, but it could be lukewarm from the heat of the sun by late afternoon. If it wasn't raining. At any time of day it was necessary to scoop out the bugs that had fallen into it before pouring some into a wash basin. A luxury they shared with six other girls was a canvas bathtub ingeniously strung up in a small copse of trees. Despite these rather crude conditions most of the hospital staff agreed that they preferred living in a tent on the side of a mountain over being billeted in the remains of some building that had survived in the town. Tents were cleaner.

They had been there for two weeks when one day Ruby broke into laughter for no apparent reason.

"What's got into you?" Catherine demanded.

"I was just thinking," Ruby managed, unable to contain her amusement, "about the Red Cross Corps brochure that lured us all into this mess. I remember thinking at the time that it sounded pretty good."

"Which one was that?" Catherine was smiling herself now, anticipating the punch line.

"You know the one. About 'an allowance of five dollars a day plus *free room and board!*'" She had to pause for a moment as another laughing fit seized her. "I never imagined that they meant five-star hotels at every stop but I sure as hell didn't picture myself like... like this!" And she doubled up with laughter, holding her sides, trying not to aggravate her tender ribcage which was finally healing from the dislocated ribs she had suffered back when they were shipping out from England.

"Oh, dear God, Ruby!" said Catherine, wiping at tears of laughter on her own cheeks, "I swear, sometimes you do have the *weirdest* sense of humour!"

The site of the hospital was surrounded by farmers' fields and it was harvest time. In the early days for those off duty it became a macabre sort of guessing game as to which innocent in which field, wanting nothing more in life than to bring in his or her crop, would be next to set off a land mine.

Alexander began his offensive on The Gothic Line stretched across northern Italy. 78 Company moved on to Mondolfo in September, through Fano, Riccione, and Rimini to Cesenatico in October. Each mile, each day, more were killed and wounded. The rains were relentless, the roads impassable, the bridges frequently washed out. Fan belts broke, tires were punctured, batteries died, tail pipes fell off. Every available billet was wet and filthy and pest ridden. Disease spread, welfare cases proliferated, court's martial became commonplace. The casualty count on both sides steadily mounted. Through it all, the unlikely romance continued.

Harold got away from his duties as often as he could. He would commandeer a vehicle, sometimes only a motorcycle, sometimes a fifteen-hundred weight or even a three-tonne lorry. Weather permitting, they would have a picnic lunch of goodies scavenged from Red Cross Packages in a shaded orange or olive grove. When the weather was inclement, they would picnic in the back of a lorry. Nobby often accompanied them. He was a wizard at preparing hot meals on the truck's engine block. On relatively warm days they might go swimming in the Adriatic, while on cooler days they might content themselves with a run along the beach or a stroll through one of the little fishing villages.

Generally speaking, the farther north they went in Italy the cleaner things got but there was also more destruction to be seen. Tempting as many of them were – luxurious private residences, for example, or small quaint hotels – they avoided using abandoned buildings for their assignations. As a few of their associates had learned the hard way too many of them were viciously booby-trapped.

As Harold's Company moved farther and farther north on Italy's east coast it became more and more difficult for him to get away for periods long enough to justify the effort. The road conditions were seldom inviting: flooded, pock-marked, washed-out, slick, muddy. One of the shortest routes was almost entirely made up of tight switchbacks, overlooking sheer drop-offs with no guard rails. On several occasions Harold made the effort nevertheless only to learn when he arrived at the hospital that Ruby had just gone back on duty or that more casualties had just been brought in so she couldn't get away. He had no choice but to turn around and go back.

They were both becoming increasingly frustrated when Ruby was once again posted the No. 4 CCS in at Cesenatico in October. This brought her much nearer to where Harold was stationed so it once again became relatively easy for him to get to her in a reasonably short space of time.

Of course, it also meant that Ruby was once more much closer to the front line and back to the grim realities of a Casualty Clearing Station with far less time off. At No. 1 CGH there were 58 nursing sisters. At No. 4 CCS there were only eight and given the necessity of working in shifts they rarely even got to see more than two or three of their coworkers. If the hours were gruelling the nature of their assignments was even more taxing. Ruby never succeeded in inuring herself completely to the ostensibly endless stream of torn, mangled, and broken bodies. And lately a more insidious fear had begun creeping into her unvoiced worries and into her troubled sleep-deprived dreams.

"What if the next one they carry in on a stretcher is... What will I do if it's Mr. Rat?"

IN THE DRAWING ROOM
October 29, 1944

Conversations in the club's drawing room were, on the whole, being conducted at a level several decibels higher than had prevailed for so many gloomy recent months. Heart-felt boisterous laughter, which had been in short supply for so long, now regularly punctuated the general cacophony. An air of expectancy prevailed. It could only be a matter of time now.

Today's dialogue between Cecil and Walter, however, was an exception. The wisdom, and perhaps more tellingly the perspective that their accumulated years had gained them, led their discussion down a darker path.

"Surely they can't *all* be megalomaniacs!" maintained Walter in a deep yearning bass. "The outcome is a foregone conclusion, even *they* must see it! Why don't they convince him to give it up?"

"Perhaps they'll have another go at assassinating him... and this time succeed!" Cecil suggested helpfully.

"Hmph!" Walter snorted. "We should be so lucky! Instead, the spineless miscreants are miring themselves in further calumny, condoning crimes against their own people. It's unthinkable, Cecil, even for them... conscripting mere children of 16 and men approaching our age into uniform! And how do they prepare these innocents for the crucible of battle, hmn? Hand the poor buggers a rifle and tell them, 'Do your duty! Defend the Fatherland!'"

"A great many of our brave lads are not much more than young boys themselves... only a couple of years older, you know," said Cecil. "Or they were at one time... young boys, I mean," he added ruefully.

Walter caught the tone. "I know what you mean, Cecil. Combat does tend to 'season' one with uncommon rapidity."

"And with precious little regard for tenderness in the process," Cecil appended. "When our fighting men return home, even those who will have yet to see their 19th birthday, they will no longer be looked upon by others... nor see themselves... as young boys."

Walter did not respond immediately. Rising ponderously, he ambled over to the sideboard and helped himself to a sausage roll. Cecil could see that his friend was chewing on something and it wasn't the greasy pastry in his hand. Cautiously lowering his great bulk into the chair, the sausage roll all but forgotten, Walter turned to Cecil with a profound look of despair. When at last he spoke, his characteristic basso profundo voice acquired peripheral intonations of doom and foreboding.

"The only question that really matters now is... how many will come home? Hmn?"

20

RIMINI TO RAVENNA, ITALY
November through December 1944

November brought thick bone-chilling fogs and torrential rains. Even 'gunfire tea,' a brew so strong it would curl your toenails, did little to ward off the chill. Harold's Company's billets at Rimini were flooded out, Harold and his men forced to sleep in the trucks. The rains soon metamorphosed into heavy, icy snowstorms transforming roads, Bailey bridges, and walkways into slick, slippery invitations to disaster. Before the month was over every third vehicle had found its way into a ditch and Ruby was among the one-in-12 sporting an elastic pressure bandage on a sprained ankle, knee, or wrist resulting from a fall.

November brought a cable informing Harold that his father, Charlie, had died on the fifth of the month. When the Colonel heard the news, he asked Harold if he would like to fill a vacancy for leave to England. Harold declined, instead nominating four other ranks as Welfare Cases deserving of home leave. Ruby tore a strip off him when she found out, but he simply patted her swelling belly and explained that he thought he could be more useful staying right where he was. He did not tell her about spending one whole evening alone sitting at the piano playing all his dad's favourite tunes well into the small hours.

November brought Catherine and heart surgeon Colonel Matt Everson to the altar. The prohibition on inter-service marriages had apparently been rescinded – whether officially or not was anyone's guess – and not surprisingly they had become an almost biweekly event. The ceremony and party were held at the officers' club in Riccione. Harold arrived as the festivities were winding up, having been run off the road by a fly-over as he was coming out of Rimini. In the past several weeks more and more units had been pulling out of Italy for service in southern France.

November brought the final push of the year for the 8th Army, now under McCreery, into Ravenna. For most of the Western World, of course, it was understood that all the 'real' fighting was now going on in northwest Europe. But in late November and early December at No. 4 Casualty Clearing Station in Cesenatico, Italy, the average number of patients that Ruby and her mates processed in a 12-hour shift climbed from 75 to 200.

IN THE DRAWING ROOM
December 30, 1944

"I am telling you, gentlemen… it's all over but the shouting!" With this unequivocal announcement, the immaculate Vice-Admiral picked up his white cotton gloves and strode purposefully from the abnormally quiet drawing room.

"Och, aye, to be sure!" murmured a Captain from the Highlanders. "Where have we hair'd *that* bullshit before?" he asked in his thick brogue of no one in particular. The small group that had formed the Vice-Admiral's impromptu audience broke up into threes and pairs. Cecil and Walter returned to their customary table.

"Well," Cecil began. "Let us hope that the Navy has the right of it and that wee Jordie over there…" Glancing over at the kilted Scot who stood at least five inches above six feet, with shoulders wider than his own considerable girth, Walter cracked a toothless smile as his friend finished.

"… is just a born pessimist."

"They are both right, of course," said Walter. "Each of them simply has a different perspective on things as they stand."

"Och, aye, to be sure!" Cecil mimicked. "That poor bastard," he said, nodding in the direction of the Highlander Captain, "will be freezing his family jewels off next week at is time somewhere in northern France or Belgium, while your comrade-in-arms will be comfortably ensconced in his cabin sipping the best cognac while his ship ferries supplies across the Channel."

"We have had this particular discussion before, Cecil," Walter responded with some irritation. "And I…"

"And you, my dear friend," Cecil was quick to forestall the imminent tirade, "have never been anything less than… I was going to say, 'sympathetic' but in justice 'empathetic' comes closer."

"Hmph!" grunted a grudgingly mollified Walter. "Well then…" he prompted. "Wishful thinking aside, how do you see it? Hmn?"

"I honestly don't know, Walter," Cecil confessed, after a moment's reflection. "I honestly do not know!"

Buskers in Rimini, Xmas Eve, 1944

VE Day (Victory in Europe) May 8, 1945

21

ITALY / ENGLAND / NETHERLANDS
December 1944 through April 1945

Ruby was going home. Well, not all the way back to Canada but as far as England at least where she had Uncle Jack and Aunt Edie and assorted cousins. What a lovely Christmas present!

She and Harold had been seeking approval for her evacuation for weeks now—ever since it had become impossible to conceal her pregnancy any longer. When approval was finally given on December 28th events moved swiftly. Her evacuation was approved but there was the problem of how to effect it. As luck would have it, Ruby's Matron was due for a rest leave and kindly volunteered to accompany her to Rome on December 29th and see what she could do to help arrange transport.

Harold went straight to Colonel Stoville and requested leave himself with the intent of seeing Ruby off. The CO was very understanding and obliged but before Harold could get away he received a note from Ruby saying that by good fortune the Matron had found her a place on a hospital ship and that she would be leaving from Naples on Wednesday, January 3rd. Chagrined but eminently practical the Colonel told Harold, "Sorry. Too late to make the trip now."

Missing her terribly already and feeling dreadfully alone and altogether miserable, Harold brightened appreciatively when a second missive arrived from Ruby on the Wednesday, her scheduled day of departure. *"My spot on ship needed for wounded man. Staying another week at least."*

He showed the note to Colonel Stoville, received a nod of approval, swapped leave vacancy with a medic he knew, and by 0330 Thursday morning he was packed and ready to depart for a five-day leave to Rome.

The car would not start. Nor the lorry. Nobby roused one of the tanker drivers and after a tow they finally got the car started at 0600. An hour later they reached Fano where they stopped for breakfast with C Platoon in the Sergeants' Mess. Heading for Macerata they made Iesi by 0900 but there they were stopped by Canadian Military Police. "No through road." Backtracking, they stopped to send a message to Ruby then started off toward Fabriano... hoping! Snow began to fall. Short of Fabriano they stopped, removed the wheels, and fitted chains. They crawled into the town around 2300 only to be told by more MPs that all the roads south or west were impassable.

After a quick bite of lunch sitting in the car, they located the traffic control officer, explained the situation and were given guarded permission to continue. Seven white-knuckled miles later they were forced to turn back. The Town Major helped them find billets. They borrowed bedding, cooked a meagre supper, and, frustrated and disappointed, went to bed early.

It came as no great surprise when the car would not start the next morning. Harold walked down the road until he found a gun truck and arranged for a tow. The car started... and stalled. Another tow. No good. They borrowed some tools and three hours later they were underway once more. And once more they were stopped by the MPs. Eventually they were allowed to go on and managed to cover 17 miles before they were stopped in their tracks until late into the afternoon. Even a snowplow got stuck.

Through pure persistence by early evening they reached Foligno by way of Fossato, gassed up and carried on. Heavy snow plagued them through Terni then turned to hard, driving rain all the way to Rome, which they finally entered near midnight. Quickly they located Canada Club but to no avail—no one there knew where Ruby was. The Town Major couldn't help them with that either, but he did get them a room at the Boston Hotel. To bed at 0100 in the morning. Two full days of his precious five-day leave *gone*.

The following morning back at Canada Club he had a stroke of good fortune. He ran into one of Ruby's mates who knew where she was billeted and before she had finished breakfast they were together again. Three glorious days to express their love for one another then he and Nobby drove back over the icy mountain roads to Cesenatico. The loneliness returned like a kick in the stomach. Cruelly, Ruby's departure was delayed until January 30th. Only a few hours' drive separated them for all the remaining long lonely days of the month.

Ruby found a berth on the Dutch hospital ship *Oranje*, and even before the ship had left the pier it was made painfully clear to her that her pregnancy had robbed her of the sea legs of which she had been so proud. Paired with the morning sickness, to which she had resigned, the gentle swells of the Mediterranean induced a persistent nausea and for two days she found that she was unable to keep down anything but very sweet tea. When the little ship reached the Atlantic and began to buck and roll in earnest, she couldn't manage even that.

Dehydrated and exhausted after what seemed like an eternity Ruby finally arrived safely at Portsmouth. After a brusque but competent examination by one of the port's resident MOs...

"How do you feel?

"Like death warmed over!"

She was given some salt pills and pronounced fit for travel. So, on February 4th she was helped onto a train and found herself in London in time for dinner at the Rembrandt Hotel where the Red Cross had arranged to put her up for the night. Next morning her Uncle Jack and Aunt Edie collected her and took her back to their cottage in Romford.

She had been nervous, not knowing what kind of reception she would be accorded, anticipating stern censure at the very least. But if Uncle and Auntie harboured any critical thoughts or feelings about the conduct or the condition of their niece it was certainly not apparent in anything they said or did. On the contrary, they treated her as if she were their own daughter (in point of fact, they had three sons), and if there was one emotion other than unqualified love manifest in their behaviour toward her, it was pride.

"A *Captain,* you say! And he's come up through the ranks!" Uncle Jack made no attempt to conceal his approval. Owing to a weak heart he had never been permitted to serve in the armed forces, but two of his three sons had come of age during the proceedings and were now in uniform. Thankfully neither had yet seen service overseas.

They were seated in the parlor of the small cottage in Romford, Uncle Jack and Aunt Edie sharing a plump overstuffed sofa upholstered in a floral design from a previous era with Ruby ensconced in a plush oversized easy chair that was normally reserved, she had no doubt, for her uncle.

"Uncle Jack, Auntie..." Ruby began, still feeling the pangs of trepidation, "I'm sure, if you could just meet him..."

"All in good time, my dear," soothed Aunt Edie, gently stroking her niece's shoulder. "All in good time."

"Oh, but honestly, he's... he's..." Ruby stammered.

"Errol Flynn? Without the Hollywood cameras?" Aunt Edie suggested.

Ruby had to laugh despite herself. "Well, if I had to compare him to a movie star then I would say more like David Niven."

"Ah!" Aunt Edie replied knowingly. "Not quite so dashing, but every inch a gentleman, is that it?"

"Oh, Auntie!" Ruby chuckled, nodding. "He most certainly is a gentleman but... I had to worm this out of him... he saw active duty with the British Commandos for almost two years so you might say he has his quota of 'dash', as well."

"For any man in uniform these days," ventured Uncle Jack, glancing back and forth between his wife and his niece, the hint of a smile tugging at the corners of his mouth, "genuine humility is even more rare than a good joint of beef."

Ruby smiled even more broadly and reached out to grasp her uncle's big callused hand. "Thank you, Uncle Jack! Your approval," and she was careful to include Aunt Edie in her gaze, "means a lot to me. It's almost as if... well, with Mom and Dad so far away..."

"We know we cannot replace them, dear," murmured Aunt Edie, taking her niece's hands between her own. "But we shall stand in for them as best we can."

Relief flooding through her, Ruby at last allowed the tears to flow. Which unfortunately induced hiccups. Which in turn threatened to bring on premature contractions that she clearly did not want or need just now. Calling upon the self-control she had worked so assiduously to master in the field hospitals, she closed her eyes and stretched both arms out in front of her, hands together, palms down. Uncle Jack and Aunt Edie exchanged looks of concern but remained silent. They could not possibly know or understand but Ruby was re-enacting in her mind's eye the test of nerves she had devised for herself at Cassino.

She pictured Catherine placing the two brim-full glasses of water on the backs of her hands. She saw herself staring at those tumblers and slowly counting to 100. She heard the rumble of the artillery shells exploding nearby and felt the ground beneath her feet vibrate with their implosions. The hiccups ceased. The tears abated. She opened her eyes and nodded reassuringly at her aunt and uncle.

"Everything's going to be alright."

Three days later, feeling somewhat restored by the tender ministrations and Aunt Edie's simple but nutritious cooking, Ruby braced herself for the next challenge. Accompanied by Colonel Stoville's wife, who had been apprised of the situation in a letter from her husband, she went up to Beckenham and met her new mother-in-law and two new sisters-in-law for the first time. The warmth of their reception quickly dispelled her lingering fears and concerns. The following weekend she was invited to stay over at Beckenham, and Violet, uncharacteristically critical of her Toddy, insisted on buying her a 'proper' wedding ring. (A simple ring of hammered pewter was all that Harold had been able to find in war-torn Italy at the time of their nuptials.)

In short, Ruby was promptly made to feel welcome by her father's brother and his family in Essex as well as by her new in-laws in Kent. She exchanged letters with Harold – sometimes writing three or more in a day or just one very long multi-paged one – to keep him posted on her situation and condition.

Yet it was in a letter from his sister Irene that Harold first learned of the birth of his son on April 17th, 1945. As he was born in his Great-Uncle Jack's house, they dubbed him "Jackie," but he was christened "John

Charles" after Ruby's brother who had been shot down over Germany and Harold's father, Charlie.

Meanwhile Harold, too, had left Italy.

On April 10th they sailed at dawn from 'Leghorn' (Livorno), arriving in Marseilles early the following morning. They literally sped through France and Belgium, arriving at and settling into Eindhoven in the Netherlands on the day of Jackie's birth, though Harold was not to learn of that happy event until Irene's letter caught up with him six days later. As fate would have it, the No. 1 CGH and No. 4 CSS were stationed in Nijmegen only a short distance away.

IN THE DRAWING ROOM
May 3, 1945

"No, I'm not really surprised, Walter. Disappointed perhaps but not surprised," said Cecil.

"Disappointed, old man?" Walter looked confused. "The blighter... the *fiend* is *dead!* And by his own hand... and his bitch mistress along with him! Even his bloody *dog* was put down, apparently. A fitting end, if you ask me!"

Cecil clenched his eyes tightly and sucked in his breath as if attempting to master by willpower alone a sudden severe abdominal cramp. "Is it 'fitting,' Walter," he asked quietly, "that a man who was almost single-handedly responsible for visiting so much pain and suffering upon the world should have been allowed to 'shuffle off this mortal coil' with so little pain or suffering of his own?"

Exhaling volubly, Cecil opened his eyes and regarded his friend with an expression both accusatory and beseeching at the same time. "Would it not have been more 'fitting', more *purgative...*" he virtually bleated, "... for his myriad victims if the monster had been brought to trial to answer for his crimes before an international tribunal?"

"You're thinking of this new, um... United Nations organization, I presume?" Walter prompted, beginning to understand where his old friend was coming from.

"That is one possibility, Walter." Cecil answered. "And if my present disposition were inclined toward the sort of fair and impartial justice for which the British system of jurisprudence is justly renowned then I would agree with you. But quite honestly fairness and impartiality hold no particular attraction for me at this juncture. No. To be perfectly frank I would have liked to see that 'little corporal' shithead tried by those against whom he and his Lieutenants perpetrated the worst atrocities!"

"The Jews, of course..." Walter offered abjectly, "and... our*selves*, perhaps. We stood alone against them for... well, I needn't tell you. And the Russians! They have also suffered horrendously!"

"By all reports," Cecil snapped, sitting bolt upright, "the Russians are exacting their 'pound of flesh' in Berlin, even as we speak! Rape and pillage, and…" Cecil's voice trailed off.

Walter reached beneath the table and placed a comforting hand on Cecil's knee. "Who, then?" he inquired softly.

"Oh, Walter!" Cecil moaned. "The surviving citizens of Germany itself, of course!" With a visible effort he collected himself.

"Can you begin to imagine their anguish, Walter? Their total despair? Their *Führer,* an undeniably charismatic head of state, had mesmerized them with his big lies into believing that they, the 'pure Aryans' – a concept which, I allow, too many of them all-too-readily embraced – were destined to rule the entire world. He promised a reincarnation of the Roman Empire, but one that would endure not for 300 years but for 3,000! Heady stuff, you know," Cecil wound down. "Oh yes, my friend," he closed, "I would have dearly loved to have seen Herr Hitler judged by his own citizens."

22

NETHERLANDS / ENGLAND / GERMANY / ENGLAND

May 1945 through November 1946

Cease-fire in Europe was declared at 0241 hours on May 8th.

With his CO and the other officers of the Company Harold listened to Churchill's speech on the radio at three o'clock that afternoon, announcing that war in Europe was over! He thanked God but couldn't seem to muster much enthusiasm.

He thought he had left the rains behind in Italy. *Hah!* He thought his migraine headaches were going to leave him alone for a while. *Hah!* He thought being so much closer to home-based supply lines that they would stand a reasonable chance of maintaining a majority of vehicles in working condition. *Hah!* He hoped once the fighting stopped that the daily pressures might slack off a little. *Hah! And wouldn't daffodils in January be lovely!*

Sooner than he had dared to hope Harold did get a brief respite. Home leave—the first in *three years!*

He was granted ten days leave. He crossed from Calais to Folkeston and took the train up to London on June 2nd. After a brief stop to see his mother and sisters in Beckenham he went down to Romford and to Ruby and to see for the first time his infant son. To say it was a happy reunion would be like saying that the sky is blue. But it was not without distractions.

Jackie was in rather a foul mood and kept them awake most nights with his crying. However, it was difficult to be cross with the poor little tyke. Everyone acknowledged that he had good reason to be upset. Just three weeks prior to his entry into this world one of the last of the V-2 rockets had landed close enough to send shrapnel through the wall and into his crib. Great Uncle Jack had not yet got around to repairing the crib so he was being put to sleep on a cushion from the sofa with books piled around it so that he would not roll off onto the floor.

There was news from Canada that Ruby's father had been discharged from the Navy because of a heart condition. There were financial matters to sort out. There was the future to consider.

Did Ruby want to stay in England? She just wanted to be with him.

Wouldn't she be happier going home to Canada? Well, yes, frankly.

Would Harold really be willing to follow her there? Naturally, but... would he be allowed to? Would he be able to find work there? Assuming, of course, that he would receive his discharge: the war might be over in Europe but there were still the Japanese and the Pacific theatre.

When all was said and done it was a very pleasant if not entirely care-free ten days before Harold had to return to Eindhoven. In that interval they accomplished a number of things. They did some shopping, mostly for baby clothes. They had Jackie's birth officially recorded at the Romford Registrar's office. Each made an effort to get to know their respective in-laws a little better. Thoroughly embarrassed by his mother's example (and a few of her more carefully chosen words spoken in front of Ruby's Uncle Jack), Harold went up to London and bought Ruby a belated engagement ring at Battersby's. He bought new frames for his spectacles, repaired his cigarette lighter and his razor, and Jackie's unfortunate crib. Ruby bought him some new sheet music. And they made love, eagerly, tenderly, repeatedly.

The aftermath of the war in Europe was, in its own ways, just as demanding as the fighting had been. The damage everywhere was mind boggling. Roads, buildings, railroad tracks, bridges, port facilities, telephone lines, sewer systems, the entire infrastructure of countries had to be put right. Shortages of virtually every commodity, especially food in the early days, took many months and thousands of labour hours to begin to alleviate. And as for the ravaged minds and broken bodies and anguished hearts of the peoples…

Ruby and Jackie arrived in Montreal on July 22nd, the same day Harold was posted to 11 Company, 30th Corps in Syke, (Seckenhausen) south of Bremen. His beloved Nobby was no longer with him having at last been promoted to Lieutenant and kept behind with 78th Company. A new batman was assigned to him – a pleasant and competent enough young man named Chuddley – but it just wasn't the same without Nobby. And the new OC, to Harold's disgust, was a recent transfer in from England, a 'desk jockey' who had never even crossed the Channel until now. Harold found him to be incompetent, puerile, and mean-spirited. He dealt with the situation – all of it – as best he could over the ensuing months. He even applied himself to learning to speak and write German and succeeded in bringing his linguistic repertoire to five.

Logistical problems continued to occupy most of his time and to demand every ounce of skill and knowledge that he could bring to bear upon them. Second only to this main activity came courts of inquiry and disciplinary issues arising from frequent, unpleasant incidents with civilians (some of whom were recently demobilized former German military men), including some in which shots were fired in anger by one side or the other. There were accusations, sometimes true, sometimes false, of theft, rape, and various other common crimes. Then there were The Python Boys, so labelled because of their too often successful efforts to 'squeeze' money or goods from civilian and military personnel alike through a protection racket, where they, of course, offered the most imminent threat of bodily harm.

He was still very much in demand whenever there was a piano or an accordion to be played. Whenever he could find time he wrote or talked to anyone and everyone he could think of about his prospects for eventually emigrating to Canada. The responses were not encouraging, particularly the official ones.

ARMY EDUCATION SCHEME
VOCATIONAL INFORMATION BULLETIN NO. 1
July 1945

CANADA

The mobilization of Canada's resources for the common war effort in some respects involved a relatively greater displacement of personnel than in most other countries. There are, for example between 300,000 and 400,000 soldiers and airmen overseas, many of whom have been away from their homes for four or five years without a break. Their repatriation and re-establishment in civilian life will be a first charge on the Government of Canada and must take priority over the movement and placement of others. Having in mind shortage of shipping, which is expected to continue for a considerable period after the end of the European hostilities and is likely to make repatriation of service personnel a disappointingly slow business, the Canadian Government does not think it is possible to give realistic consideration at this time to possible plans for the movement of other classes of persons. In this connection it is also pointed out that the great expansion of war industries in Canada has tended to be concentrated in certain areas, to which scores of thousands of workers have been drawn from all over the country. Here again the task of their establishment in normal civilian employments will be of considerable magnitude and is likely to take some time.

These problems are therefore receiving priority in the Canadian Government's consideration. As the Government makes progress with the question of repatriation and re-establishment of Canadian overseas service personnel and of the demobilization of war industries, they will be ready to consider with other countries what steps should be taken to facilitate the movement of persons wishing to change their place of work and residence from one country to another. They have examined the conditions under which reciprocal exchange of social security benefits can be arranged in such cases and other kindred aspects of the subject. They will gladly enter discussions with the United Kingdom authorities on these matters as early as the situation may make this practicable and fruitful.

Finally, the 'desk jockey' botched matters so badly he was shipped home. It was difficult to say who was more pleased to see his backside, the soldiers who had had to put up with his daily incompetence or the locals whom he had treated with contempt. With his departure Harold was promoted to Major and appointed Officer Commanding on November 30th. One of the first orders he issued was for the release and distribution of foodstuffs to the citizens of Seckenhausen who were quite literally starving to death. Over the next ten days he devoted a great deal of his time and energy to establishing viable working relationships with the local political leaders. That he was successful to a degree was evident in the marked and sustained diminution in crime and complaints against the occupying forces.

The exigencies of his position were often so impracticable as to be intimidating. Yet, he was grateful for them. The more his attention had to be focused on the task at hand the less time he spent dwelling on the pain of separation from Ruby and Jackie. The moon here didn't look at all as it had on the beach at Rimini. So why did it make him think of that far away evening when they had sat in the front of a lorry smoking cigarettes, looking out at the sea, and talking quietly about their future? Surely rain was just rain, no matter where or when it fell. Why then could he not listen to the susurrous droplets without being reminded of her?

Winter settled in making even minor chores more difficult and the lonely nights longer. Everything needed was in short supply but food, in particular, had to be rationed with untenable stringency. Even on the black market the only commodity that could be found dependably was American cigarettes. Belligerence once more reared its ugly head on all sides. Verbal squabbles quickly degenerated into slugfests or worse. Disgruntled locals vented their anger in acts of sabotage or for the bolder among them, hooliganism. For many, thievery became the only means of survival.

Harold urged the civil authorities to show the thieves – those who were after food – compassion, but for those who stole anything else at all and for the saboteurs and the rowdies he felt no such compunction. He was adamant that they be dealt with summarily and severely which, he hoped, would send a clear message to anyone contemplating a similar course of action. For the most part he had his way, but whether that was because the civilians sitting in judgment of their own people agreed with his position or because they were simply being compliant because they were dependent on his goodwill he couldn't decide.

The Company's strength bloated to 506 and transfers in and out were constant as various units were being disbanded and more and more men and women were 'demobbed.'

Suddenly, it was Harold's turn.

He was released on January 22nd, 1946 and officially demobilized on January 25th exactly five years and five months after having been called to the colours. By April he was back working at Barclay's Bank in the branch on Mount Street off Park Lane for the princely sum of £330 per annum. All too soon he was bored silly.

He exhausted every conceivable avenue in his efforts to gain permission to emigrate to Canada. He even went so far as to apply for a visa to the United States of America, reasoning that at least that would get him closer to Ruby and Jackie. It was a time-devouring totally frustrating process consisting mostly of one failed initiative after another, nearly all of which began and ended with "wait and see." This waiting time he filled with make-work projects around the house in Beckenham. There were plenty of them because so many things had not been attended to since Charlie's death. A steady stream of letters and care packages arrived from Canada almost daily and he did his best to respond in kind. His mother and sisters were always there for him and one or another frequently made time to accompany him down to Romford to take tea with 'Auntie and Uncle Cobbett,' and to keep them apprised of news from Ruby, especially where it concerned Jackie.

The months passed. Work at the bank was tedious and unrewarding despite two quick promotions and corresponding rises in salary. All of the red tape and bureaucratic mumbo jumbo involved in his emigration pursuits increasingly weighed upon him, but he never gave up trying and hoping, and ultimately, he was rewarded with a temporary visa to Canada. Somehow, he was determined, he would stay in Canada once he got there. So he resigned from the bank, packed and crated everything he owned (most importantly, his sheet music and his accordion), and had it shipped from Liverpool on a cargo ship, supposedly to be delivered to him in Hamilton within a few days of his own arrival.

Sailing from Southampton by way of Cherbourg on the *S. S. Aquitania* – crammed in seven to a cabin deep below decks – his ship docked at Pier 90 in New York at 5:00 p.m. on November 2nd.

Ruby was there to greet him.

IN THE DRAWING ROOM
September 3, 1945

"They call them DPs, you know. Stands for 'displaced persons.'" Cecil said quietly.

"I don't like it," grumbled Walter. "Has a pejorative ring to it. It's not their fault that they're homeless, penniless, and starving! Why can't they just call them refugees, hmn?"

"I don't know, Walter. Seems this war has added a lot of new words to our vocabulary, like..." Cecil thought for a moment, scratching his head. "Like *Blitzkrieg* and *concentration camp* and *buzz bomb* and *kamikaze*... frightening concepts even to contemplate."

"Especially for the next generation," said Walter.

Cecil almost smiled at that. "So, Julia and Major Buchkowsky will live in the United States after they're married?"

Walter nodded. "And raise beautiful babies... in the dreadful shadow of the Atomic bomb."

On Leave - H.S.L. meets Jackie

Major Harold Stanley Lawes, 1945

Mr. & Mrs. Rat back in uniform, 1952

ACKNOWLEDGEMENTS

My parents shared a mutual, understandable reluctance to respond directly to the inevitable question: "And what did *you* do in the war?"

Happily for all concerned, they loved to entertain and often among the guests would be those whom I came to think of as 'special people.' People who, like my parents, had been there. Occasionally some of these special people would stay very late into the evening and they and my parents would all get into their cups and start reminiscing or trading – quite literally – war stories.

My baby sister Gina would have been asleep in her crib and I, it would have been presumed – this would have been in the early to mid-50s – was similarly out of harm's way. Sitting in my pajamas at the top of the stairs, 'out of sight, out of mind,' I thus overheard any number of hair-raising narratives and soul baring confessions. Looking back, I wonder that I did not suffer from constant nightmares but I suppose, to my child's mind, the horrors being spoken of so calmly and matter-of-factly in my parents' living room never put on the cloth of reality. Or not until much, much later in any event. I have incorporated a few of those stair-top anecdotes into this story: the laundry hampers, and the night-time Gurkha raid, both near Monte Cassino, for example (Chapter 16.) I will leave it to the reader's imagination to discern where else in the manuscript the details provided might be attributable to the humbly spoken words of heroes... as overheard by a child almost 70 years ago.

Cheers!

CPSIA information can be obtained
at www.ICGtesting.com
Printed in the USA
BVHW041026031220
594764BV00006B/100